ROUTLEDGE LIBRARY EDITIONS: COMEDY

Volume 11

COMEDY

COMEDY

L. J. POTTS

Routledge
Taylor & Francis Group
LONDON AND NEW YORK

First published in 1949 by Hutchinson & Co (Publishers) Ltd

This edition first published in 2022
by Routledge
4 Park Square, Milton Park, Abingdon, Oxon OX14 4RN

and by Routledge
605 Third Avenue, New York, NY 10158

Routledge is an imprint of the Taylor & Francis Group, an informa business

© 1949

All rights reserved. No part of this book may be reprinted or reproduced or utilised in any form or by any electronic, mechanical, or other means, now known or hereafter invented, including photocopying and recording, or in any information storage or retrieval system, without permission in writing from the publishers.

Trademark notice: Product or corporate names may be trademarks or registered trademarks, and are used only for identification and explanation without intent to infringe.

British Library Cataloguing in Publication Data
A catalogue record for this book is available from the British Library

ISBN: 978-1-032-20971-5 (Set)
ISBN: 978-1-032-21133-6 (Volume 11) (hbk)
ISBN: 978-1-032-21136-7 (Volume 11) (pbk)
ISBN: 978-1-003-26691-4 (Volume 11) (ebk)

DOI: 10.4324/9781003266914

Publisher's Note
The publisher has gone to great lengths to ensure the quality of this reprint but points out that some imperfections in the original copies may be apparent.

Disclaimer
The publisher has made every effort to trace copyright holders and would welcome correspondence from those they have been unable to trace.

COMEDY

L. J. Potts
late Fellow of Queens' College, Cambridge

HUTCHINSON UNIVERSITY LIBRARY
LONDON

HUTCHINSON & CO (*Publishers*) LTD
178–202 Great Portland Street, London W1

London Melbourne Sydney
Auckland Bombay Toronto
Johannesburg New York

*First published 1949
Second impression 1957
Third impression 1960
Fourth impression 1966*

The paperback edition of this book is sold subject to the condition that it shall not, by way of trade or otherwise, be lent, resold, hired out, or otherwise circulated without the publisher's prior consent in any form of binding or cover other than that in which it is published and without a similar condition including this condition being imposed on the subsequent purchaser

This book has been set in Fournier, printed in Great Britain on Smooth Wove paper by Anchor Press, and bound by Wm. Brendon, both of Tiptree, Essex

CONTENTS

	Preface	7
1	Introduction	9
2	The idea of comedy	14
3	Subject matter	41
4	Style	58
5	Character and plot	96
6	The boundaries of comedy	128
	Notes	145
	Bibliographical Index	151
	General Index	157

'Men have been wise in very different modes; but they have always laughed the same way.'
SAMUEL JOHNSON

'With the ancients, and not less with the elder dramatists of England and France, both comedy and tragedy were considered as kinds of poetry. They neither sought in comedy to make us laugh merely, much less to make us laugh by wry faces, accidents of jargon, slang phrases for the day, or the clothing of commonplace morals in metaphors drawn from the shops of mechanic occupations of their characters; nor did they condescend in tragedy to wheedle away the applause of the spectators, by representing before them fac-similes of their own mean selves in all their existing meanness, or to work on their sluggish sympathies by a pathos not a whit more respectable than the maudlin tears of drunkenness.'
SAMUEL TAYLOR COLERIDGE

'It is only by unremitting effort that we can persist in being individuals in a society, instead of merely members of a disciplined crowd. Yet we remain members of the crowd, even when we succeed in being individuals.'
T. S. ELIOT

PREFACE

This book is not a history of Comedy, or even of English Comedy; but I have tried to give it something of a historical character by a bibliographical index, and to illustrate it fully and widely by quotations from English comic writers. I have modernised the spelling and punctuation of the earlier writers, except Chaucer. Chaucer cannot be modernised, and I was unwilling to translate him; I assume that any of my readers who have no previous acquaintance with his English will sufficiently understand, from the context, what I have quoted from him. I have occasionally italicised a part of a quotation without apology.

So far as I know the theories contained in this book are part of the stock-in-trade of modern criticism, deriving mainly from Aristotle and Coleridge. I have explained my method at the beginning of chapter 6. I am indebted to the Editor of the English Literature section of this series for inviting me to write this particular book; and to him and to the Master of Jesus College in this University for valuable advice and for much enlightenment and stimulus from their writings. Miss Rosemary Beresford has done me the great kindness of reading the book chapter by chapter in manuscript, and her acute and constructive criticisms have enabled me to correct several errors of judgment. My wife has also read the book in manuscript, and many of the ideas in it reached their present form in discussion with her.

In view of the continued demand for the book, it seemed best to the publishers and the author to reprint it without change, except that the deaths of Bernard Shaw and Max Beerbohm have made it necessary to add two dates to the Bibliographical Index. The author takes this opportunity to pay tribute to their memory.

Queens' College, Cambridge
August 1957

I

INTRODUCTION

Of all kinds of literature comedy has the widest appeal. Wit and humour can bridge the deepest intellectual and even emotional chasms; they can create, if only for a moment, the completest harmony between men who are violently and angrily opposed to each other in politics, morality, and even character. At the same time it is true that the sense of humour varies from man to man very greatly, both in degree and in kind. It is a faculty that we can discover, with a little patience, in most people, perhaps in everybody; but like most other human faculties it is not highly developed at birth, and we cannot keep it active in ourselves, or respond to it in other people, without an effort of imagination. Humour is a kind of poetry. It springs, spontaneous and complete, from and into the mind; but it does not thrive in idle heads or in the company of undisciplined feelings.

In the foregoing paragraph I have vaguely identified comedy with wit and humour. There are dangers in doing so. Comedy must be thought of as an art form: as a way of writing; or, since it is not confined to literature, a way of drawing, or dancing, and so forth. We often describe episodes or people in real life as comic because they happen to appeal to our sense of humour. But nothing in nature is positively and categorically comic: whether it is so depends on how you look at it, or to be more precise, what you make of it. (Max Beerbohm has an enlightening essay on this subject in *Yet Again*, 'The Humour of the Public'). Of course there is no harm in extracting comedy from life; but there is harm in mistaking our extract for the real thing. What we see may be comic, but we never see the whole of anything; if we saw more, or with a clearer vision, the comedy might turn to tragedy; and even then the thing itself would not be tragic. The importance of this somewhat pedantic distinction is two-fold. It is a principle of humanity and good manners, as anyone who has laughed too hastily (even to himself) can appreciate. But it is also a crucial principle of aesthetics: for the first stage in every art is perception, or vision, or imagination, and whenever we perceive or imagine we are potential artists, even if we do not go on to communicate our vision to other people in what is called creative art.

In classifying comedy as an art-form I must draw another distinction. Some literary forms, such as the lyric, the novel, or drama, depend on outward shape or size: a lyric, for instance, is a short poem based on the pattern of a song. The difference between a short story and a novel is comparable to the difference between, say, a cottage and a hotel. But there is another kind of difference in architecture exemplified in the contrast between a cathedral and a town hall: the difference between ecclesiastical and civic architecture, which is a difference in function, intention, or point of view. Comedy is one of the few art-forms that are defined by that kind of distinction. Its outward shape is variable; it can be narrative, dramatic, or descriptive; the most amorphous of literary vehicles, the essay, suits it admirably; it can occur without words at all—in picture, sculpture or ballet. By tradition and by nature it is, however, most at home in literature; and I shall treat it as a literary form. But since it is distinguished from most of the literary forms by its philosophy rather than its structure, I shall call it a *mode of thought*; by which I mean that its character depends on the attitude of the writer to life.

There are only two literary modes of thought: tragedy and comedy. The nearest other species of literature to these two is the epic; but epic has never had a philosophical character so clearly defined as that of tragedy and comedy. It seems to be in a class halfway between the modes of thought and the purely structural forms. It is not quite a contradiction in terms to speak of a tragic epic or a comic epic, and if we can do so, then the epic is not parallel to, but intersects, these modes. In spite of a persistent feeling among writers that there is such a thing as an epic or heroic mode of thought, the epic has not evolved: it has remained primitive and incalculable. Nor again is satire a species of the same order as tragedy and comedy: one can speak of satirical comedy. It seems that we classify a work as satirical in virtue of its practical purpose, rather than its quality of thought or feeling. Tragedy and comedy are, however, strictly parallel, both in their history and in their character as fully developed conventions of art; and in attempting to explain the one we are constantly driven to compare and contrast it with the other.

There is an eclectic form of fiction, borrowing certain of the superficial or accidental features of tragedy and comedy, but containing none of the essence of either, and lacking both their pedigree and their philosophical justification: tragicomedy. Dryden defended it; it has a popular appeal, and has commended itself to dramatists who like to please their public. There is no great harm in a play or novel that pains and frightens us superficially and not in full earnest, adding yet another thrill—of artificial felicity—by an inappropriate stroke of good fortune in the last act or chapter. But it is not the happy ending that makes a comedy; nor merely the pity and fear that make a tragedy. Therefore, despite this apparent exception to the rule, I propose to treat tragedy and comedy as distinct and mutually exclusive modes.

I have used metaphors from biology: 'evolution' and 'pedigree'. Such metaphors are always suspect. But in using them I wished to imply that literature and literary forms, as also language and linguistic forms, not only develop (which is obvious), but grow in a way that is comparable to biological evolution. The history of science records the accumulating achievements of the mind of man; but in language and literature we have, as it were in fossil form, the development of that mind itself not merely from millennium to millennium, but from century to century or even lifetime to lifetime. It is true that language and literature can be regarded simply as one of the products of man; as part of our invented machinery for making life easier, safer, pleasanter, and more comfortable. According to this view they are to be judged simply by their efficiency as means to a variety of ends: and the older forms of literature, having served their purpose, should be replaced by more powerful products of inventive resourcefulness, as the stage-coach has been replaced by the express train. The history of literary criticism is largely influenced by various versions of this doctrine: perhaps the most celebrated example in England is Peacock's *Four Ages of Poetry*, which applied it to poetry as a whole. Many people believe that the growth of the novel has made the epic unreadable; and that the elaborate arts of Greek tragedy and medieval allegory have no significance for the twentieth century. In his very interesting essay *Tragedy and the Whole Truth* Aldous Huxley suggests that tragedy may be out of date; but he reprieves her at the last moment on the ground that she is too valuable to be allowed to die.

The mechanistic view of literature is equally unfavourable to the survival of comedy; and it cannot be countered by a mere assertion of values. But it is an unscientific view. In fact literature is always renewing its strength from the inspiration of its older forms: ours has done so in every century from the sixteenth to the twentieth. And of course the mind of man itself is not, like its inventions, constantly being *replaced*; it is like the trunk of a tree, whose new growths do not eliminate but *contain* all the earlier stages of its growth. And I think it is now generally recognised that whatever the end of art may be, its forms grow rather than are made. Comedy and tragedy might have been invented at a fairly advanced stage of civilisation (say by Aristotle or Sophocles or Aristophanes); but in fact they were not. They grew gradually out of something more primitive: and it is significant that they grew out of two different primitive activities. The origins of poetry, drama, and prose fiction cannot be traced to a single source; but the clear distinction between comedy and tragedy comes from ancient Athens, where they first appeared as fully organised art-forms. At Athens there was an official state theatre to gather together the most fruitful expressions of native feeling and imagination within the framework of national festivals; and in the fifth century B.C. much of the energy and originality of the Athenian mind went into art and particularly drama. We can watch the growth of tragedy in the plays of three great dramatists over three-quarters of a century; and we are watching not merely or even mainly the creative activity of three writers of genius, but the development of a national mind in all its preoccupations: religious, philosophical, political and domestic, as well as aesthetic. Two thousand years later, in a very different emotional and intellectual atmosphere and under conditions much less favourable to the dramatic artist, our own Shakespeare, and to a lesser extent the other dramatists of his period, poured the English national mind into the same vessel of tragedy: essentially the same vessel, though very different superficially. English tragedy was a native growth, but it was not a native invention; the plays of the

Introduction

Latin philosopher Seneca, themselves modelled on the form of Greek tragedy, were well known to the Elizabethans and served in their turn as a model to give shape to our tragedy in its early stages. Thus tragedy grew and modified itself with the growth and modifications of the human mind: and it went on growing, to include the great tragedies of Racine in seventeenth-century France, and Ibsen and Strindberg in nineteenth-century Scandinavia.

The survivals of early comedy are not so rich or comprehensive. The Athenians found that tragedy was inadequate to express their national life, and in the course of time they included a complementary art-form in their dramatic festivals. In its primitive origins comedy is as old and goes as deep as tragedy; but it is more irreverent and it was slower to win official recognition. It is to the credit of the Athenians that by the middle of the fifth century comedy had taken its place by the side of tragedy. The range of Aristophanes is as wide as that of Aeschylus, but his spirit and tendency are utterly different, though obviously a manifestation of the same age and locality. Greek comedy went on developing long after the development of Greek tragedy was complete; and again it served as a model for the Romans (Plautus and Terence), and they in their turn served as models for our Elizabethan dramatists. And so onwards, to Molière and Bernard Shaw.

In this country, which had no organised State theatre, the evolution of comedy had to be worked by the originality of individual writers. But long before the time of Shakespeare there was a vigorous English comic tradition. It flowered, with brilliance unequalled to this day, in Chaucer; and we possess a primitive but artistically excellent example of the (mainly oral) medieval comic tradition, in *The Second Shepherd's Play* of the Towneley series of miracle plays. Comedy, like tragedy, is a Greek word, and so far as any people may claim to have invented the two modes the Athenians must be given the credit; but clearly they are natural activities of man, not invented by anyone but arising out of the quality of the human mind.

2

THE IDEA OF COMEDY

I

I do not propose to define comedy in so many words. It would not be possible to find any but a vague formula to fit *The Birds* of Aristophanes, *Tristram Shandy, A Midsummer Night's Dream*, and *Pride and Prejudice*. Moreover, to give definition to an art-form is the business of the artist, and not of the critic; for the artist it is all-important to work within strict limits, but for his public and his critics it is equally important not to be tied to formulae. To the reader of comedy, who has the finished product, the recipe counts for little; and this is true of all art in a sense in which it is only partly true of ethics. Moreover, though definitions, like creeds, tell us a great deal about the people who make them, they are seldom completely valid for anyone else. In his famous definition of tragedy, Aristotle limits it to the drama, because in his day tragedy was the name of a branch of drama; it is no longer thus limited. He also ascribes to it a particular moral effect, which was very likely its effect on him and quite possibly its effect on most of his contemporaries; but our ethical tradition is different from Aristotle's and it is not now generally true that tragedy *liberates* the mind of pity and fear. We all need to be able to make definitions, in order to clear our own heads and explain to other people what we mean by words of vague or variable meaning; but as the starting-point of discussion, they often hinder understanding more than they help it.

Yet something may be said about the end of comedy; and by 'end' I mean not its moral purpose or its commercial value, but its philosophical and psychological character. About this I believe Meredith, in his *Essay on Comedy*, written seventy years ago, was

The idea of comedy

right in the main, though his style jars somewhat on the twentieth-century ear, and though he disparages the English genius for comedy with a quite inexplicable perversity, I find little to quarrel with in his analysis of the Comic Spirit:

> If you believe that our civilisation is founded in common-sense (and it is the first condition of sanity to believe it), you will, when contemplating men, discern a Spirit overhead; not more heavenly than the light flashed upward from glassy surfaces, but luminous and watchful; never shooting beyond them [*i.e.* men] nor lagging in the rear; so closely attached to them that it may be taken for a slavish reflex, until its features are studied. It has the sage's brows, and the sunny malice of a faun lurks at the corners of the half-closed lips drawn in an idle wariness of half tension. That slim feasting smile, shaped like the long-bow, was once a big round satyr's laugh, that flung up the brows like a fortress lifted by gunpowder. The laugh will come again, but it will be of the order of the smile, finely tempered, showing sunlight of the mind, mental richness rather than noisy enormity. Its common aspect is one of unsolicitous observation, as if surveying a full field and having leisure to dart on its chosen morsels without any fluttering eagerness. Men's future upon earth does not attract it; their honesty and shapeliness in the present does; and whenever they wax out of proportion, overblown, affected, pretentious, bombastical, hypocritical, pedantic, fantastically delicate; whenever it sees them self-deceived or hoodwinked, given to run riot in idolatries, drifting into vanities, congregating in absurdities, planning shortsightedly, plotting dementedly; whenever they are at variance with their professions, and violate the unwritten but perceptible laws binding them in consideration to one to another; whenever they offend sound reason, fair justice; are false in humility or mined with conceit, individually, or in the bulk—the Spirit overhead will look humanely malign and cast an oblique light on them, followed by volleys of silvery laughter. That is the Comic Spirit.

II

I connect the essential distinction between tragedy and comedy with two opposing impulses deeply rooted in human nature. Until we can find a way of reconciling the antinomy in our nature we are all torn between the desire to *find* ourselves and the desire to *lose* ourselves. It is on some such antithesis as this that Coleridge based his whole philosophy, and in particular his theory of imagination.

We are impelled to preserve and accentuate and glory in our

separate lives; we believe that every member of our species has his particular and distinct destiny; there are even atheists who cannot bring themselves to believe in the possibility of their own extinction. This natural pride of man and in man I believe to be the psychological foundation of tragedy. It may seem strange that tragedies should always end with disaster and usually in death; why should we read books or go to the theatre in order to make ourselves miserable? Is it not morbid and even rather immoral to encourage in ourselves and other people a despairing and defeatist view of life? Jane Austen, with her invariable and refreshing freedom from cant, puts this point of view in a famous sentence in *Mansfield Park*: 'Let other pens dwell on guilt and misery; I quit such odious subjects as soon as I can.' And even so great a philosopher as Plato objected to tragedy for the same reason, among others. But surely the answer is obvious. We cannot see human nature in its full pride and glory until it is isolated, stripped of all its comforts and protections, left face to face with its most powerful enemies; and that is how we see the great tragic heroes—Prometheus and Medea, Hamlet and Lear. Indeed it is here that the test of tragedy lies: if it does, in the end, make us miserable, if the view of life that it proclaims seems to us defeatist, then either it has failed to achieve its end, or we have failed to respond properly to it. If on the other hand we reach a conclusion like Shelley's at the end of *Prometheus Unbound*, then we are receiving the proper effect of tragedy:

> To suffer woes which Hope thinks infinite;
> To forgive wrongs darker than death or night;
>   To defy Power, which seems omnipotent;
> To love, and bear; to hope till Hope creates
> From its own wreck, the thing it contemplates;
>   Neither to change, nor falter, nor repent;
> This, like thy glory, Titan, is to be
> Good, great and joyous, beautiful and free;
> This is alone Life, Joy, Empire and Victory.

But if there is a proper human pride, there is also a proper human modesty; and the two are never, I think, far from each other. We cherish our separateness jealously; but we need also to merge it in the life of the world into which we were born, to mix with other people, to adjust our own wills and even our characters to the *milieu* in which by choice or necessity we live and to the general

The idea of comedy

laws of nature. This second impulse is surely as healthy and strong as the other, and it is found in men of the most vigorous and robust character; Blake, for instance, cries in one of his most moving lines

'O why was I born with a different face?'

We cannot be satisfied with the mere assertion of our individuality; we must recognise a destiny other than our individual destinies: the destiny of our race. From one point of view every sparrow is infinitely important; from another the greatest man is completely unimportant. These two truths are complementary, and perhaps neither has much meaning without the other. This is one of the great paradoxes of the Christian religion; but one does not need to be a Christian to recognise its truth.

The conviction that the individual is unimportant except as a part of something wider; the impulse to mix, and to seek common ground with the rest of one's kind; social sense; these have their proper expression in art as well as in religion. In art it is not, as a rule, so exalted; but perhaps it is equally effective. When this tendency is uppermost in our minds we look upon our abnormal traits of character not as precious possessions to be clung to through life and death, but as eccentricities; not as part of our destiny, but as essentially detached from it, for are we not essentially men and women like our neighbours? It is to this notion that I shall refer all that I have to say in support of the somewhat strict theory of comedy I wish to advocate.

In contrast to the stricter notions of comedy the general English notion is vague and fluid. If a play, especially at its end, gives us pleasant feelings about life, our programmes label it a comedy. In the stock modern 'comedy' we expect a rather sugary and enervating love interest. The popular idea of comedy can be summed up in two simple notions.

The first is that if a play makes you laugh it is a comedy. Obviously laughter has something to do with comedy; and therefore most of the philosophical attempts to analyse comedy have centred in discussions of laughter and its causes. Laughter is an odd human habit, and it has not unnaturally attracted the attention of philosophers and psychologists; though there is something incongruous about lengthy and patient investigations of it, and their conclusions are unsatisfying—for example, that it is an expression of cruelty, or a signal of defeat. I cannot help thinking that to identify comedy with laughter is to begin at the wrong end. Laughter is a physical act, and if we try to trace its causes to a single source they will lead us very far from drama or literature. As Shylock says, 'if you tickle us, do we not laugh?' Or again, most people agree that they are prone to laughter at funerals and on other solemn occasions; it is common for a man to laugh violently in the presence of horror, or under the influence of sudden grief. These are the most natural, perhaps the only completely natural, kinds of laughter. On the other hand our laughter at what we suppose to be funny is often quite conventional. In the essay to which I have referred, Max Beerbohm made a list of the recurring themes at which the comic papers of that time invited their readers to laugh, beginning of course with mothers-in-law; and of such laughter one need seek no further cause than that people have agreed that at a certain signal they may or should laugh. About the subject matter of comedy I shall say something in the next chapter; but the subjects of comedy are not to be identified with the causes of laughter.

The fact is that laughter is a very erratic and unreliable action, ranging from the hysterical scream or giggle to the deliberate trumpeting of disapproval or discontent, and from the loud guffaw of the vacant mind to an utterly peaceful signal of sudden sympathy or complete understanding. Moreover it is very doubtful whether the end of comedy is to produce laughter. Many of the greatest comedies have a rather sobering effect, which has led to very confusing conclusions: such as the conclusion that high comedies like *Don Quixote*, *The Tempest*, and *Le Misantrope* are tragedies. Shakespeare's contemporaries no doubt laughed heartily at the ill-treatment of Malvolio in the last two acts of *Twelfth Night*; we are mostly too uncomfortable to do so, but we are not therefore to conclude either that our sense of comedy is defective or that Malvolio is a tragic figure. The truth is that just as the emotions evoked by tragedy are too complex to be called merely sad, so comedy is too complex to be merely funny. I am content to note that laughter is one of the means by which the comic writer seeks to influence his public, whatever his end may be. It is true that we laugh spontaneously at any one or any happening that strikes us as eccentric—off the highway of normal human life. This may well be the only essential link between laughter and comedy.

The other popular notion is that any play with a happy ending is

The idea of comedy

a comedy. This is open to similar objections. To begin with, happiness is so wide and vague a term that it introduces rather than removes confusion. The conventional end of a tragedy is the death of the hero (or some catastrophe approximating to death), and the conventional end of a comedy is a wedding. But supposing Shakespeare had kept Hamlet and Ophelia alive and married them off at the end of the play, he would not thereby have turned it into a comedy; or again, Alceste in Molière's *Misantrope* does not marry either Célimène or Eliante, but that does not turn the play into a tragedy, though it is sometimes shallowly said to do so; nor is *Volpone* a tragedy, although it ends in the ruin and imprisonment of the hero.

Behind this notion there is a full-fledged fallacy: a confusion between art and its raw material. For good reasons, into which I will go later, a certain kind of plot is appropriate to tragedy and a different kind to comedy; hence has arisen the convention of ending tragedies with death and comedies with marriage. But death by itself is not tragic: when a reporter describes a street accident as a 'tragic fatality' simply because somebody is killed, he is misusing language. It is even possible to treat death comically; Charles II made comedy of his own death; and though it is perhaps somewhat indecent to apply comic wit to real death, no such objection can be made about its application to deaths in fiction. There is the death of Jim who was eaten by a lion in Hilaire Belloc's *Cautionary Tales*: and there is Brown's death in Max Beerbohm's story '*Savonarola' Brown* in *Seven Men*:

> 'But in a tragedy,' I insisted, 'the catastrophe *must* be led up to, step by step. My dear Brown, the end of the hero *must* be logical and rational.'
> 'I don't see that,' he said, as we crossed Piccadilly Circus. 'In actual life it isn't so. What is there to prevent a motor-omnibus from knocking me over and killing me at this moment?'
> At that moment, by what has always seemed to me the strangest of coincidences, and just the sort of thing that playwrights ought to avoid, a motor-omnibus knocked Brown over and killed him.

This not only illustrates, but also explains, the point I am trying to make.

In any case, 'happy' and 'unhappy' are very inappropriate words in this connexion. When Milton writes, at the end of *Samson Agonistes*:

> Nothing is here for tears, nothing to wail
> Or knock the breast, no weakness, no contempt,
> Dispraise, or blame, nothing but well and fair . . .

he is not saying 'This play is a comedy'. And as for marriage: examine the end of any good comedy that leads up to a wedding—*Much Ado about Nothing*, *The Way of the World*, *Pride and Prejudice*, *Major Barbara*. The happiness is irrelevant, though it may be present. The point is that all these comedies end in a question mark: the one thing certain is that a wedding is not the end but the beginning of a story. This inconclusiveness at the end of many comedies has an important bearing on the nature of plot in comedy. And it is often extremely disquieting, and sometimes profoundly sad, marriage or no marriage.

The end of a play or a novel is indeed important; but it must be appropriate to the rest of the plot. It does not *by itself* determine the character of the work. Dr Johnson disposed neatly of the 'happy ending' fallacy in his Preface to Shakespeare:

> The players, who in their edition divided our author's works into comedies, histories, and tragedies, seem not to have distinguished the three kinds by any very exact or definite ideas.
> An action which ended happily to the principal persons, however serious or distressful through its intermediate incidents, in their opinion constituted a comedy. This idea of a comedy continued long amongst us; and plays were written which, by changing the catastrophe, were tragedies today and comedies tomorrow.

In spite of Johnson, the idea still continues amongst us.

III

It is easier to form a concept from examples than from abstract formulae. I will therefore extract four scenes from four English works as diverse as possible: *A Midsummer Night's Dream*, *Tristram Shandy*, *Emma*, and *Major Barbara*. I have deliberately chosen well-known comedies, and from those comedies the most obvious scenes I could find for my purpose, since I want to focus attention on specimens of a class of literature with which the English reader is familiar enough, rather than to make any new

The idea of comedy

discoveries. It will be necessary to quote at length and in full, in order to give our authors sufficient room to deploy their forces, and in order to have their actual words under our eyes; for in comedy, as in all other highly developed forms of literature, single words are important, but they are only important in a wide context. Certainly, a handful of examples cannot prove any theory; but they can explain and give reality to it.

First, a part of Act III, scene i of *A Midsummer Night's Dream*, where Titania awakes under the spell and falls in love with Bottom. Just before the extract begins Bottom has appeared on the stage with his ass's head on, and his companions have fled in terror.

BOTTOM I see their knavery: this is to make an ass of me; to fright me, if they could. But I will not stir from this place, do what they can: I will walk up and down here, and I will sing, that they shall hear I am not afraid.

> *The ousel cock so black of hue,*
>   *With orange-tawny bill,*
> *The throstle with his note so true,*
>   *The wren with little quill ...*

TITANIA What angel wakes me from my flowery bed?

BOTTOM
> *The finch, the sparrow, and the lark,*
>   *The plain-song cuckoo gray,*
> *Whose note full many a man doth mark,*
>   *And dares not answer Nay ...*

—for indeed, who would set his wit to so foolish a bird? who would give a bird the lie, though he cry 'cuckoo' never so?

TITANIA I pray thee, gentle mortal, sing again:
Mine ear is much enamoured of thy note;
So is mine eye enthralled to thy shape;
And thy fair virtue's force perforce doth move me
On the first view to say, to swear, I love thee.

BOTTOM Methinks, mistress, you should have little reason for that: and yet, to say the truth, reason and love keep little company together nowadays; the more the pity, that some honest neighbours will not make them friends.
Nay, I can gleek upon occasion.

TITANIA Thou art as wise as thou art beautiful.

BOTTOM Not so neither: but if I had wit enough to get out of this wood I have enough to serve mine own turn.

TITANIA Out of this wood do not desire to go;
         Thou shalt remain here whether thou wilt or no.
         I am a spirit of no common rate;
         The summer still doth tend upon my state;
         And I do love thee. Therefore go with me;
         I'll give thee fairies to attend on thee,
         And they shall fetch thee jewels from the deep,
         And sing, while thou on pressed flowers dost sleep,
         And I will purge thy mortal grossness so,
         That thou shalt like an airy spirit go. . . .

The appeal of this scene is immediate and universal, but it is extremely complex. To begin with, the sight of a man with a donkey's head on him is funny. Incongruity provokes laughter. But mere physical incongruity is not comedy, any more than physical horrors are tragedy. This kind of sensationalism, which we call farce when it is ludicrous, and which is sometimes (inaccurately) called melodrama when it is gruesome, is not of itself either comic or tragic. Yet a comedy may contain farce, and comedy may even be embedded in farce (as here); it is none the worse for that. Shakespeare, who liked to appeal to his audiences at different levels and made it his business to master every kind of dramatic and theatrical effect, relied much on farce for provoking an immediate response in his audience: for administering the first shock.

But the donkey's head is more than a stage property: it is a symbol. For the good-natured but thoughtless and innocent weaver is an ass; he can even miss the point of the time-honoured joke about cuckolds. Shakespeare indeed rather labours his point, with somewhat obvious comic irony: 'this is to make an ass of me'. Bottom has already unconsciously called attention to his 'translation'. When Snout says 'O Bottom, thou art changed! What do I see on thee?' he answers, 'What do you see? You see an ass-head of your own, do you?'; and now he takes the ass-head to himself, still unconsciously. The simplest minds in the audience see the point and are delighted with the play and with themselves.

The incongruity between the confidence of Bottom's manner and the absurdity of his appearance makes good low comedy. But the main point of the scene lies of course not in the simplicity of Bottom but in the fatuity of the exquisite Titania. Every word she speaks is ridiculous: especially her application to Bottom of the word 'gentle', which still in Shakespeare's time had its older meaning, of the

The idea of comedy

nobility of mind and body belonging to high-bred men and animals. Not only so, but the whole style of her speeches (the artificial, mannered, and high-flown metre, rhythm, and diction of Elizabethan romantic verse) is almost pathetically ludicrous in its context. Considering for a moment the play as a whole, this deterioration in the fairy mentality has already been foreshadowed by the foolish squabble over the page-boy and by the Oberon-Puck muddle over the love-charm; the fairies are charming, graceful, powerful, and even well-meaning, but how childish and inefficient!

At this point Bottom comes into his own: his world is at least self-sufficient within its humble limits. To Titania's declaration of love he makes a sensible reply, no more original than one would expect, but adequate to the situation. And then he properly changes the subject, referring back to her compliment on his singing. This calls forth an even more ludicrous compliment, for once in straightforward language: 'Thou art as wise as thou art beautiful'. Taken literally this is perhaps true; but Bottom is not in the least put out: he caps it with a piece of real, if homespun, wisdom.

It is in the way in which Bottom and Titania throw each other into relief that the high comedy of the scene consists. When, in the very next scene, Puck makes his famous comment on mankind, 'Lord, what fools these mortals be!' one may miss the irony. Fools we are, but there is something more foolish than natural human folly. And even Puck, the best of the fairies, has, to use Bottom's words, little reason for his gibe.

The antithesis between Titania and Bottom is at the heart of comedy; Shakespeare repeats it in many variations (Malvolio and Sir Toby Belch; Don John and Dogberry; and the entire collection of characters in *As You Like It*, from the two Dukes with their heads full of fancies about life, to the empty-headed Audrey, secure and self-sufficient in her exuberant sluttishness). But all the great comic writers make much of it: Chaucer, for instance, in the contrast between the Prioress and the Wife of Bath, or between January and May in the Merchant's Tale; Cervantes in the immortal partnership of Don Quixote and Sancho Panza; Fielding repeatedly (as when Tom Jones falls plumb out of his lofty rhapsody on Sophia's virtues and charms into the arms of Molly Seagrim, or when he discovers the philosopher Square squatting on his hams behind the curtain in Molly's bedroom). It is on his perception of this duality in human nature and the imagination with which he dramatises it again and again that Bernard Shaw's reputation as a comic writer chiefly rests.

This is the main significance of *A Midsummer Night's Dream*. It is a profound revelation of human nature: of the paradox by which extreme fastidious refinement exists in us side by side with the vulgarest fleshly processes and propensities. Shakespeare was a dramatist as well as a poet, and he mastered the art of the theatre early in his career; Titania and Bottom are fully developed personalities; but more than this—they are symbols. There is irony in Titania's speech beginning 'Out of this wood do not desire to go . . .' She is truly a spirit of no common rate; but neither she, nor any spirit, can purge our mortal grossness, and if she could we should not be the better for it. In all of us there is both a Titania and a Bottom (and with what genius Shakespeare named the two characters!).

Here, then, we reach that poetical comedy which sets Shakespeare apart from most dramatists and above all others. This scene, ranging from crude farce to high poetical comedy, tells us all we need to know about the comic mode. But comparatively little comedy is on this level. More commonly its scenes are closer to ordinary life. Almost always it hints at the fundamental human inconsistency between the ideal and the reality; but it also depicts every variety of clash between contrasting ideas and temperaments. Of this more quotidian comedy there is no better example than *Tristram Shandy*. Sterne's inconsequential manner of telling a story, and his somewhat irritating habit of leaving gaps, marked by asterisks, to be filled in by the reader's imagination, make it difficult to detach any passage that does him full justice; but here is a scene from Volume v, chapters 31 and 32, clearly showing the characters of four of the main persons: Walter Shandy ('my father'), his brother Toby, Toby's servant Corporal Trim, and the parson Yorick. Walter Shandy is holding forth about the authority of parents over their children.

'I enter upon this speculation,' said my father carelessly, and half-shutting the book, as he went on—'merely to shew the foundation of the natural relation between a father and his child; the right and jurisdiction over whom he acquires these several ways—
1st, by marriage.
2nd, by adoption.
3rd, by legitimation.
And 4th, by procreation; all which I consider in their order.'

'I lay a slight stress upon one of them,' replied Yorick;—'the act, especially where it ends there, in my opinion lays as little obligation upon the child, as it conveys power to the father.'

'You are wrong,' said my father, argutely, 'and for this plain reason * * * * * *. —I own,' added my father, 'that the offspring, upon this account, is not so under the power and jurisdiction of the *mother*.'

'But the reason,' replied Yorick, 'equally holds good for her.'

'She is under authority herself,' said my father: 'and besides,' continued my father, nodding his head and laying his finger upon the side of his nose, as he assigned his reason, '*she is not the principal agent*, Yorick.'

'In what?' quoth my uncle Toby, stopping his pipe.

'Though by all means,' added my father (not attending to my uncle Toby), '*The son ought to pay her respect*, as you may read, Yorick, at large in the first book of the Institutes of Justinian, at the eleventh tide and the tenth section.'

'I can read it as well,' replied Yorick, 'in the Catechism.'

'Trim can repeat every word of it by heart,' quoth my uncle Toby.

'Pugh!' said my father, not caring to be interrupted with Trim's saying his Catechism.

'He can, upon my honour,' replied my uncle Toby. 'Ask him, Mr Yorick, any question you please.'

'The Fifth Commandment, Trim,' said Yorick, speaking mildly, and with a gentle nod, as to a modest catachumen.

The Corporal stood silent.

'You don't ask him right,' said my uncle Toby, raising his voice, and giving it rapidly like the word of command: 'The Fifth!' cried my uncle Toby.

'I must begin with the First, an't please your Honour,' said the Corporal.

Yorick could not forbear smiling.

'Your Reverence does not consider,' said the Corporal, shouldering his stick like a musket, and marching into the middle of the room, to illustrate his position, 'that 'tis exactly the same thing as doing one's exercise in the field.'

'*Join your right hand to your firelock!*' cried the Corporal, giving the word of command, and performing the motion.—'*Poise your firelock!*' cried the Corporal, doing the duty still of both adjutant and private man. —'*Rest your firelock!*'—one motion, an't please your Reverence, you see, leads into another. If his Honour will begin but with the First——'

'*The First!*' cried my uncle Toby, setting his hand upon his side. . . . '*The Second!*' cried my uncle Toby, waving his tobacco-pipe, as he would have done his sword at the head of a regiment. . . . The Corporal went through his *manual* with exactness; and having *honoured his father and mother*, made a low bow, and fell back to the side of the room.

'Every thing in the world,' said my father, 'is big with jest,—and has wit in it, and instruction too,—if we can but find it out. Here is the *scaffold-work* of *Instruction,* its true point of folly, without the *building* behind it.—Here is the glass for pedagogues, preceptors, tutors, governors, gerund-grinders, and bear-leaders to view themselves in, in their true dimensions.—Oh! there is a husk and shell, Yorick, which grows up with learning, which their unskilfulness knows not how to fling away! *Sciences may be learned by rote, but Wisdom not.*'

Yorick thought my father inspired.

'I will enter into obligations this moment,' said my father, 'to lay out all my aunt Dinah's legacy in charitable uses' (of which, by the bye, my father had no high opinion) 'if the Corporal has any one determinate idea annexed to any one word he has repeated. Prithee, Trim,' quoth my father, turning round to him, 'what dost thou mean by *honouring thy father and mother?*'

'Allowing them, an' please your Honour, three halfpence a day out of my pay, when they grow old.'

'And didst thou do that, Trim?' said Yorick.

'He did indeed,' replied my uncle Toby.

'Then, Trim,' said Yorick, springing out of his chair, and taking the Corporal by the hand, 'thou art the best commentator upon that part of the Decalogue; and I honour thee more for it, Corporal Trim, than if thou hadst had a hand in the Talmud itself.'

The effect of this passage is less concentrated and complex than that of the Bottom-Titania scene: but it is admirably controlled. Sterne had a genius for imagining and revealing the working of simple minds in their social actions and reactions, and for building up a scene, largely in dialogue, out of these alone. In spite of Yorick's last speech (which is strictly in character) the scene is not moral in intention or effect. It is a display of morally neutral characteristics.

These two passages are both funny; but explaining jokes is always thankless, and having explained Shakespeare's in great detail I do not think it necessary to say more at present about Sterne's. But comedy is not always laughing matter, and I add two scenes, the one from Jane Austen, the other from Bernard Shaw, depicting more or less painful situations.

The first comes from *Emma,* and is the famous climax of the book in chapter 47. The heroine, Emma Woodhouse, is talking to her protégée, Harriet Smith, whom she supposes to have suffered a disappointment at the news that Frank Churchill is engaged to Jane Fairfax.

'I never had the slightest suspicion, till within the last hour, of Mr Frank Churchill's having the least regard for Jane Fairfax. You may be very sure that, if I had, I should have cautioned you accordingly.'

'Me!' cried Harriet, colouring, and astonished. 'Why should you caution me? You do not think I care about Mr Frank Churchill?'

'I am delighted to hear you speak so stoutly on the subject,' replied Emma, smiling; 'but you do not mean to deny that there was a time—and not very distant either—when you gave me reason to understand that you did care about him?'

'Him!—never, never. Dear Miss Woodhouse, how could you so mistake me?' (turning away distressed).

'Harriet,' cried Emma, after a moment's pause, 'what do you mean?—Good Heaven! What do you mean?—Mistake you!—Am I to suppose then——?'

She could not speak another word. Her voice was lost; and she sat down, waiting in great terror till Harriet should answer.

Harriet, who was standing at some distance, and with face turned from her, did not immediately say anything; and when she did speak, it was in a voice nearly as agitated as Emma's.

'I should not have thought it possible,' she began, 'that you could have misunderstood me! I know we agreed never to name him—but considering how infinitely superior he is to everybody else, I should not have thought it possible that I could be supposed to mean any other person. Mr Frank Churchill, indeed! I do not know who would ever look at him in the company of the other. I hope I have a better taste than to think of Mr Frank Churchill, who is like nobody by his side. And that you should have been so mistaken is amazing!—I am sure, but for believing that you entirely approved and meant to encourage me in my attachment, I should have considered it at first too great a presumptoin almost to dare to think of him. At first, if you had not told me that more wonderful things had happened; that there had been matches of greater disparity (those were your very words)—I should not have dared to give way to—I should not have thought it possible;—but if *you*, who had been always acquainted with him——'

'Harriet,' cried Emma, collecting herself resolutely, 'let us understand each other now, without the possibility of farther mistake. Are you speaking of—Mr Knightley?'

'To be sure I am. I never could have an idea of anybody else—and so I thought you knew. When we talked about him, it was clear as possible.'

'Not quite,' returned Emma, with forced calmness; 'for all that you then said appeared to me to relate to a different person. I could almost assert that you had *named* Mr Frank Churchill. I am sure the service Mr Frank Churchill had rendered you, in protecting you from the gipsies, was spoken of.'

'Oh, Miss Woodhouse, how you do forget!'

'My dear Harriet, I perfectly remember the substance of what I said on the occasion. I told you that I did not wonder at your attachment; that, considering the service he had rendered you, it was extremely natural;—and you agreed to it, expressing yourself very warmly as to your sense of that service, and mentioning even what your sensations had been in seeing him come forward to your rescue. The impression of it is strong on my memory.'

'Oh, dear,' cried Harriet, 'now I recollect what you mean; but I was thinking of something very different at the time. It was not the gipsies—it was not Mr Frank Churchill that I meant. No!' (with some elevation), 'I was thinking of a much more precious circumstance—of Mr Knightley's coming and asking me to dance, when Mr Elton would not stand up with me, and when there was no other partner in the room. That was the kind action; that was the noble benevolence and generosity; that was the service which made me begin to feel how superior he was to every other being upon earth.'

'Good God!' cried Emma, 'this has been a most unfortunate—most deplorable mistake! What is to be done?'

'You would not have encouraged me, then, if you had understood me? At least, however, I cannot be worse off than I should have been, if the other had been the person; and now—it *is* possible——'

She paused a few moments. Emma could not speak.

'I do not wonder, Miss Woodhouse,' she resumed, 'that you should feel a great difference between the two, as to me or as to anybody. You must think one five hundred million times more above me than the other. But I hope, Miss Woodhouse, that supposing—that if—strange as it may appear——. But you know they were your own words, that *more* wonderful things had happened; matches of *greater* disparity had taken place than between Mr Frank Churchill and me; and, therefore, it seems as if such a thing even as this may have occurred before—and if I should be so fortunate, beyond expression, as to—if Mr Knightley should really—if *he* does not mind the disparity, I hope, dear Miss Woodhouse, you will not set yourself against it and try to put difficulties in the way. But you are too good for that, I am sure.'

Harriet was standing at one of the windows. Emma turned round to look at her in consternation, and hastily said,

'Have you any idea of Mr Knightley's returning your affection?'

'Yes,' replied Harriet, modestly but not fearfully; 'I must say that I have.'

Emma's eyes were instantly withdrawn; and she sat silently meditating, in a fixed attitude, for a few minutes. A few minutes were sufficient for making her acquainted with her own heart. A mind like hers, once opening to suspicion, made rapid progress. She touched, she admitted

The idea of comedy 29

she acknowledged the whole truth. Why was it so much worse that Harriet should be in love with Mr Knightley than with Frank Churchill? Why was the evil so dreadfully increased by Harriet's having some hope of a return? It darted through her with the speed of an arrow that Mr Knightley must marry no one but herself!

Her own conduct, as well as her own heart, was before her in the same few minutes. She saw it all with a clearness which had never blessed her before. How improperly had she been acting by Harriet! How inconsiderate, how indelicate, how irrational, how unfeeling, had been her conduct! What blindness, what madness had led her on! It struck her with dreadful force, and she was ready to give it every bad name in the world. Some portion of respect for herself, however, in spite of all these demerits, some concern for her own appearance, and a strong sense of justice by Harriet (there would be no need of *compassion* to the girl who believed herself loved by Mr Knightley—but justice required that she should not be made unhappy by any coldness now), gave Emma the resolution to sit and endure farther with calmness, with even apparent kindness. For her own advantage, indeed, it was fit that the utmost extent of Harriet's hopes should be enquired into; and Harriet had done nothing to forfeit the regard and interest which had been so voluntarily formed and maintained, or to deserve to be slighted by the person whose counsels had never led her right. Rousing from reflection, therefore, and subduing her emotion, she turned to Harriet again, and in a more inviting accent renewed the conversation; for as to the subject which had first introduced it, the wonderful story of Jane Fairfax, that was quite sunk and lost. Neither of them thought but of Mr Knightley and themselves.

There is nothing to laugh at in this scene; it is entirely serious. The drama is tense, and the style acquires a corresponding tension:

She could not speak another word. Her voice was lost; and she sat down, waiting in great terror till Harriet should answer....

'Yes,' replied Harriet, modestly but not fearfully; 'I must say that I have.'

To be sure, in spite of this, it is not tragic. Though the situation is both painful and critical, it is in no way abnormal: just an accident, such as stupidity and ignorance of the world on one side, and hastiness and self-conceit on the other, might cause at any time. And though Emma rises to the occasion she does not rise above it; she is brave and self-possessed, but no more heroic than common sense warrants. 'Mr Knightley must marry no one but herself.' 'There would be no need of *compassion* to the girl who believed herself loved by Mr Knightley—but justice required that she should not be made unhappy by any coldness now . . .' 'For her own advantage, indeed, it was fit that the utmost extent of Harriet's hopes should be enquired into.' Most revealing of all, her kindness for Harriet has ceased to be more than 'apparent'. In all this there is no grandeur; nothing on the heights; no more than may be expected of average humanity. But in what sense can it be called comic?

I have challenged this question. The general effect of comedy is to relax tension of feeling; but it has its moments of tension, and I wished to instance one of them. This illustrates the unsatisfactoriness of judging any book by extracts, or even judging any part of a book out of its widest context. To do so is like attempting to judge a man's isolated speeches or acts without reference to the rest of his life. Yet, when we know a man's character thoroughly, everything he says or does becomes for us characteristic; and this should be even truer of a work of art, since a work of art should be even more homogeneous than nature—everything in it should contribute to the total effect. The important questions, then, will be first, whether *Emma* as a whole is a comedy, and secondly, whether the passage I have quoted from it is out of keeping, in the place in which it occurs, with the rest of the book. Obviously, neither of these questions can be answered from the extract by itself. But for my present purpose I will assume that the passage is in keeping, and that the novel as a whole is a comedy. If these assumptions are correct, we ought to be able to detect the quality of comedy in this scene, although perhaps it is not very noticeable. I think we can.

To begin with, the two characters show each other up. Harriet betrays her helplessness and dependence on Emma both in the manner and in the matter of every word she speaks, except her last dramatic sentence: particularly in her pathetic appeal to Emma not to interfere between her and Mr Knightley. She has no imagination, and only that kind of intelligence that can distort everything to agree with whatever idea or emotion has possession of her. It has never occurred to her to wonder whether she would be a success as Mr Knightley's wife; she admits the disparity between them, yet the farthest reach her imagination can carry to is the notion (derived from something Emma has said) that Mr Knightley and Emma might overlook it. But her very passivity and unintelligence make her the more effective as a foil to Emma. The irony of the whole situation is fairly obvious, and Emma sees it when she admits that

The idea of comedy

Harriet 'does not deserve to be slighted by the person whose counsels had never led her right'. It was Emma who had first made Harriet see herself as a person of consequence; she had persuaded Harriet to refuse Robert Martin's offer of marriage because he was only a small farmer, and had encouraged her twice to aim at more ambitious matches. She has even to admit that Harriet's infatuation for Mr Knightley might have been harmless but for her own blunder in unconsciously sanctioning it. And two things that Harriet says show Emma up even more completely. 'Mr Frank Churchill, indeed! I do not know *who would ever look at him in the company of the other*': but Emma herself had done precisely that—she had flirted with Frank, and even toyed (though not seriously) with the notion of marrying him, but she had never till now thought of marrying Mr Knightley. And again it was the unintelligent Harriet who realised (by intuition) that Mr Knightley's dancing with her was a 'much more precious circumstance' than Frank's rescuing her from the gipsies. So twice in this scene Harriet shows that her values have been right while Emma's have been wrong. Jane Austen is too good an artist to call attention to this; but it has its effect in convincing Emma that she has been not only inconsiderate and indelicate, but *irrational* and *unfeeling*.

Greater stress, however, is laid upon Emma's virtues than upon her faults. While Harriet gives herself away without reflexion and without restraint, Emma can hold her tongue and think. While Harriet drifts further and further into delusion, Emma's first question as soon as she discovers what has happened, is 'What is to be *done*?' Throughout this scene her mind always pushes forward one stage ahead of her knowledge; and this lively imagination, which has been the chief source of her errors, is now a source of strength. 'A mind like hers, once opening to suspicion, made rapid progress.' In the last two paragraphs Jane Austen shows her seeing the truth both about her past conduct and about her future destiny; repenting, but with no loss of the self-respect to which she is entitled; and recovering control of the situation. In a few moments she emerges into maturity; she lives through more real experience than she has lived through in the whole of the rest of the book; she puts her past behind her and her future is assured. All that remains to be cleared up is Mr Knightley's state of mind, which both Emma and Harriet have misjudged.

It is in the clear differentiation between the two characters, thrown into relief by the dialogue and developed in the narrative, that the comedy consists. Most of it is to be found in the last two paragraphs; for comedy can be embodied in the thoughts of a single character as well as in dialogue and action. This is the advantage of the novel. In drama, for the most part, we have to deduce this internal comedy, though it can be depicted by means of soliloquy: as in Benedick's speech in Act II, scene iii of *Much Ado about Nothing*, quoted on page 81.

For my last example I will return to drama and come nearer to our own time: to Shaw's play *Major Barbara*. The scene is taken from Act II, where Barbara leaves the Salvation Army after it has been bought up by her father, Undershaft, the millionaire munition maker, and even Adolphus Cusins (who is in love with her) has gone over to the enemy under the spell of Undershaft's demonic energy and intellect.

MRS BAINES Barbara: Jenny: I have good news: most wonderful news [*Jenny runs to her*]. My prayers have been answered. I told you they would, Jenny, didnt I?
JENNY Yes, yes.
BARBARA [*moving nearer to the drum*] Have we got money enough to keep the shelter open?
MRS BAINES I hope we shall have enough to keep all the shelters open. Lord Saxmundham has promised us five thousand pounds——
BARBARA Hooray!
JENNY Glory!
MRS BAINES —if—
BARABARA 'If'! If what?
MRS BAINES —if five other gentlemen will give a thousand each to make it up to ten thousand.
BARBARA Who is Lord Saxmundham? I never heard of him.
UNDERSHAFT [*who has pricked up his ears at the peer's name, and is now watching Barbara curiously*] A new creation, my dear. You have heard of Sir Horace Bodger?
BARBARA Bodger! Do you mean the distiller? Bodger's whisky!
UNDERSHAFT That is the man. He is one of the greatest of our public benefactors. He restored the cathedral at Hakington. They made him a baronet for that. He gave half a million to the funds of his party: they made him a baron for that.
SHIRLEY What will they give him for the five thousand?
UNDERSHAFT There is nothing left to give him. So the five thousand, I should think, is to save his soul.

The idea of comedy

MRS BAINES Heaven grant it may! Oh Mr Undershaft, you have some very rich friends. Cant you help us towards the other five thousand? We are going to hold a great meeting this afternoon at the Assembly Hall in the Mile End Road. If I could only announce that one gentleman had come forward to support Lord Saxmundham, others would follow. Dont you know somebody? couldnt you? wouldnt you? [*her eyes fill with tears*] oh, think of those poor people, Mr Undershaft: think of how much it means to them, and how little to a great man like you.

UNDERSHAFT [*sardonically gallant*] Mrs Baines: you are irresistible. I cant disappoint you; and I cant deny myself the satisfaction of making Bodger pay up. You shall have your five thousand pounds.

MRS BAINES Thank God!

UNDERSHAFT You dont thank me?

MRS BAINES Oh sir, dont try to be cynical: dont be ashamed of being a good man. The Lord will bless you abundantly; and our prayers will be like to a strong fortification round you all the days of your life. [*With a touch of caution*] You will let me have the cheque to shew at the meeting, wont you? Jenny: go in and fetch a pen and ink. [*Jenny runs to the shelter door.*]

UNDERSHAFT Do not disturb Miss Hill: I have a fountain pen. [*Jenny halts. He sits at the table and writes the cheque. Cusins rises to make more room for him. They all watch him silently.*]

BILL [*cynically, aside to Barbara, his voice and accent horribly debased*] What prawce Selvytion nah?

BARBARA Stop. [*Undershaft stops writing; they all turn to her in surprise.*] Mrs Baines: are you really going to take this money?

MRS BAINES [*astonished*] Why not, dear?

BARBARA Why not! Do you know what my father is? Have you forgotten that Lord Saxmundham is Bodger the whisky man? Do you remember how we implored the County Council to stop him from writing Bodger's Whisky in letters of fire against the sky; so that the poor drink-ruined creatures on the embankment could not wake up from their snatches of sleep without being reminded of their deadly thirst by that wicked sky sign? Do you know that the worst thing I have had to fight here is not the devil, but Bodger, Bodger, Bodger, with his whisky, his distilleries, and his tied houses? Are you going to make our shelter another tied house for him, and ask me to keep it?

BILL Rotten dranken whisky it is too.

MRS BAINES Dear Barbara: Lord Saxmundham has a soul to be saved, like any of us. If heaven has found the way to make good use of his money, are we to set ourselves up against the answer to our prayers?

BARBARA I know he has a soul to be saved. Let him come down here and I'll do my best to help him to his salvation. But he wants to send his cheque down to buy us, and go on being as wicked as ever.

B

UNDERSHAFT [*with a reasonableness which Cusins alone perceives to be ironical*] My dear Barbara: alcohol is a very necessary article. It heals the sick——
BARBARA It does nothing of the sort.
UNDERSHAFT Well, it assists the doctor: that is perhaps a less questionable way of putting it. It makes life bearable to millions of people who could not endure their existence if they were quite sober. It enables Parliament to do things at eleven at night that no sane person would do at eleven in the morning. Is it Bodger's fault that this inestimable gift is deplorably abused by less than one per cent of the poor? [*He turns again to the table; signs the cheque; and crosses it.*]
MRS BAINES Barbara: will there be less drinking or more if all those poor souls we are saving come tomorrow and find the doors of our shelters shut in their faces? Lord Saxmundham gives us the money to stop drinking—to take his own business from him.
CUSINS [*impishly*] Pure self-sacrifice on Bodger's part, clearly! Bless dear Bodger! [*Barbara almost breaks down as Adolphus, too, fails her.*]
UNDERSHAFT [*tearing out the cheque and pocketing the book as he rises and goes past Cusins to Mrs Baines*] I also, Mrs Baines, may claim a little disinterestedness. Think of my business! think of the widows and orphans! the men and lads torn to pieces with shrapnel and poisoned with lyddite! [*Mrs Baines shrinks; but he goes on remorselessly*] the oceans of blood, not one drop of which is shed in a really just cause! the ravaged crops! the peaceful peasants forced, women and men, to till their fields under the fire of opposing armies on pain of starvation! the bad blood of the fierce little cowards at home who egg on others to fight for the gratification of their national vanity! All this makes money for me: I am never richer, never busier than when the papers are full of it. Well, it is your work to preach peace on earth and goodwill to men. [*Mrs Baines's face lights up again.*] Every convert you make is a vote against war. [*Her lips move in prayer.*] Yet I give you this money to help you to hasten my own commercial ruin. [*He gives her the cheque.*]
CUSINS [*mounting the form in an ecstasy of mischief*] The millennium will be inaugurated by the unselfishness of Undershaft and Bodger. Oh be joyful! [*He takes the drumsticks from his pocket and flourishes them.*]
MRS BAINES [*taking the cheque*] The longer I live the more proof I see that there is an Infinite Goodness that turns everything to the work of salvation sooner or later. Who would have thought that any good could come out of war and drink? And yet their profits are brought today to the feet of salvation to do its blessed work. [*She is affected to tears.*]
JENNY [*running to Mrs Baines and throwing her arms around her*] Oh dear! how blessed, how glorious it all is!
CUSINS [*in a convulsion of irony*] Let us seize this unspeakable moment.

Let us march to the great meeting at once. Excuse me just an instant. [*He rushes into the shelter. Jenny takes her tambourine from the drumhead.*]
MRS BAINES   Mr Undershaft: have you ever seen a thousand people fall on their knees with one impulse and pray? Come with us to the meeting. Barbara shall tell them that the Army is saved, and saved through you.
CUSINS [*returning impetuously from the shelter with a flag and a trombone, and coming between Mrs Baines and Undershaft*] You shall carry the flag down the first street, Mrs Baines [*he gives her the flag*]. Mr Undershaft is a gifted trombonist: he shall intone an Olympian diapason to the West Ham Salvation March. [*Aside to Undershaft, as he forces the trombone on him*] Blow, Machiavelli, blow.
UNDERSHAFT [*aside to him, as he takes the trombone*]   The trumpet in Zion! [*Cusins rushes to the drum, which he takes up and puts on. Undershaft continues, aloud*] I will do my best. I could vamp a bass if I knew the tune.
CUSINS   It is a wedding chorus from one of Donizetti's operas; but we have converted it. We convert everything to good here, including Bodger. You remember the chorus. 'For thee immense rejoicing—immenso giubilo—immenso giubilo' [*with drum obbligato*]. Rum tum ti tum tum, tum tum ti ta——
BARBARA   Dolly: you are breaking my heart.
CUSINS   What is a broken heart more or less here? Dionysus Undershaft has descended. I am possessed.
MRS BAINES   Come, Barbara: I must have my dear Major to carry the flag with me.
JENNY   Yes, yes, Major darling.
CUSINS [*snatches the tambourine out of Jenny's hand and mutely offers it to Barbara*]
BARBARA [*coming forward a little as she puts the offer behind her with a shudder, whilst Cusins recklessly tosses the tambourine back to Jenny and goes to the gate*] I cant come.
JENNY   Not come!
MRS BAINES [*with tears in her eyes*]   Barbara: do you think I am wrong to take the money?
BARBARA [*impulsively going to her and kissing her*] No, no: God help you, dear, you must: you are saving the Army. Go; and may you have a great meeting!
JENNY   But arnt you coming?
BARBARA   No. [*She begins taking off the silver S brooch from her collar.*
MRS BAINES   Barbara: what are you doing?
JENNY   Why are you taking your badge off? You cant be going to leave us, Major.
BARBARA [*quietly*]   Father: come here.
UNDERSHAFT [*coming to her*]   My dear! [*seeing that she is going to pin the badge on his collar, he retreats to the penthouse in some alarm.*]

BARBARA [*following him*] Dont be frightened. [*She pins the badge on and steps back towards the table, shewing him to the others.*] There! It's not much for £5000, is it?
MRS BAINES   Barbara: if you wont come and pray with us, promise me you will pray for us.
BARBARA   I cant pray now. Perhaps I shall never pray again.

This scene is even harder to assess. There is strong and obvious humour in it (for instance, Cusins's speech: 'The millennium will be inaugurated by the unselfishness of Undershaft and Bodger', the effect of which is ludicrous rather than satirical): and there is farce, when Cusins thrusts the trombone on Undershaft; yet these elements in the scene are outweighed by its underlying seriousness. The humour and farce are scarcely comic; they serve (like the so-called 'comic' relief of tragedy) as an irritant, to accentuate rather than relax the tension; they recall the bitter jests of the fool in *King Lear*. The rather crude irony of Undershaft introduces much incidental satire, on titles, alcohol, doctors, Parliament, and war: some of these themes recur in Shaw's plays with a frequency that suggests obsession. Yet the satire in this scene seems out of place, for the total effect is not satirical. Barbara's denunciation of whisky advertisements is straightforward propaganda; but it is strictly in character, and it is undermined as we realise that Barbara's own position is untenable. She herself appears as an almost tragic figure: standing bravely not only against all the other characters, but against the whole organisation of the world in which she lives. Without any doubt she appeals to the sympathies of the audience. It is, however, necessary to add that I have ended my extract with her most 'tragic' speech: from this point onwards she finds her place in the world, completely recovering her poise and confidence by the end of the play.

I have claimed that my notion of comedy is strict, and I know that I run a certain risk in selecting this scene as one of four specimens of comedy. But I believe that all of Shaw's plays, except a few 'problem plays' such as *Widowers' Houses*, are comedies; and that Shaw can only be understood if he is regarded as a writer of comedy. I shall return to him in a later chapter; for the present I leave his scene where it stands with two comments. First, like Shakespeare he is the reverse of priggish or pedantic in his notions of artistic propriety, though he has not Shakespeare's advantage

The idea of comedy 37

(or, if you like, excuse) of being one of the world's greatest poets. He is ready to work with any tools that come to his hand. He attacks his audience wherever he can see an opening; and though he keeps his end steadily in view, the means he uses go to almost any length in gratifying the tastes of the public to which he wishes to appeal: *not* a public of aesthetes, scholars, or literary critics. The lack of 'art' with which Ben Jonson reproached Shakespeare has been vindicated, and I have little doubt that Shaw's will be vindicated too, when time has placed him in perspective.

The other point I want to make here is that his comedy is of a special kind—it is the best known example in England of that kind: the comedy of ideas, which may easily be confused with something that is not comedy at all—'problem' or propagandist fiction. Shaw is not concerned primarily with ethics, as the Comedy of Humours is; nor, primarily with psychology, as the Comedy of Manners is. What he is fundamentally concerned with is ideas: the workings of human intelligence, brought to bear on the world we live in. It is Barbara's position, while she is still wavering between an ideal of self-fulfilment and one of self-abnegation, that is questionable: not her character. Both she and Cusins have failed to understand the implications of their own temperaments at the beginning of the play; their philosophies are therefore false. But the circumstances in which the dramatist places them, and the characters with which he endows them, allow them to adapt their point of view (or rather their two points of view, for Barbara is a Christian and Cusins a humanist). The characters of Shaw's men and women (unlike Jane Austen's) are rigid; this makes them potentially tragic, but Shaw's passionate belief in human intelligence gives them a freedom of action that keeps his plays within the strict limits of comedy.

IV

In his book on *The Comedy of Manners*, John Palmer refers to Horace Walpole's epigram that this world is a comedy to those that think and a tragedy to those that feel, and expands it thus:

The swelling of human passion and the clash of emotion may for the spectators at a play be either comic or tragic. If the author has presented them so that the audience is invited to look upon them at a distance, if he makes his appeal to the intelligence rather than to the sympathy of his hearers, he is making the comic appeal.

To explain the relevance of this notion we may contrast the Titania-Bottom scene with another Shakespearean scene where crudity and delicacy are shown side by side, the scene where Othello is strangling Desdemona. Here we have two dramatisations of the same fundamental human antinomy. In *A Midsummer Night's Dream* there is a clear-cut discrimination between the characters; Titania and Bottom belong to different planes of reality, so that if the scene is to be dramatic at all a symbolism almost as precise as that of allegory must be ascribed to it. In *Othello* the effect is merely emotional; Shakespeare's only purpose is to distress us. But if we feel any distress or disgust at the sight of Titania embracing Bottom, then surely our sense of comedy is defective; unless indeed Shakespeare himself has made an error of taste and is lacking in true discrimination, which I will not admit. Some slight sadness there may be in perceiving the incompatibilities of human nature and the un-ideal character of life; but this is a sadness of the intellect.

Nor does the passage from *Tristram Shandy* appeal to emotion; it invites us to meditate on the oddities of human nature and the paradox by which the actions of the simple-minded often weigh more heavily in the scale than the wisdom of the learned. But with the scene from *Emma* we are on more difficult ground. It is impossible not to share the feelings of the two girls; and if it were possible, it would not be right. Indeed in all her novels Jane Austen appeals to our sympathy as she traces the fortunes of her heroines: to say nothing of Fanny Price and Anne Elliot, if we cannot feel with, as well as for, Catherine Morland and Elizabeth Bennet and Emma in their mistakes and frustrations, our reading of these books is insensitive and shallow. So too in *Major Barbara* one feels for the heroine. And in the greatest comedy the feeling can be intense: in *Don Quixote*, for example, and in Molière's most moving play *Le Misantrope*. So Horace Walpole's *mot* should not be pressed to its logical conclusion: in fact, of course, intellect cannot be thus isolated from emotion.

But comedy does keep our sympathies under strict control, and in due time withholds them. If Bottom had been at all a repulsive or malicious character, we might have overbalanced into partisanship on Titania's behalf; but Shakespeare's tact is such that we feel she is well matched—Bottom is neither more nor less than she deserves. Oberon might feel differently; but then he was not impartial; he was a fairy too, and had not been behaving any better than she had; his conscience was not clear, and perhaps his marital vanity was touched by the exhibition of his Queen in such an undignified plight. As for Sterne, he distributes the honours between his characters with a most exact sense of proportion. Walter Shandy takes the lead: it is his nature so to do. But Yorick, though he 'thought my father inspired', has the last word twice in this short scene; and as I have already said, the simplicity of Toby and Trim is too much for Walter's philosophy. Indeed there is a rough correspondence between the Walter-Toby situation and the Titania-Bottom situation; Walter's intellectualism parallels Titania's exquisiteness, and the simplicity of Toby's question 'In what?' is very similar to that of Bottom's comment on the cuckoo song.

Jane Austen has an equally good sense of proportion. We sympathise with both Emma and Harriet; and if our sympathy with Emma is the greater, it is partly because she is bearing a double burden of responsibility and mortification, and partly because she herself is capable of stronger and more complicated feelings than Harriet is. Nothing is accorded to, or withheld from, either of them, except what is precisely due to their characters; and it is commendable in Jane Austen that she has not ascribed to Harriet the smallest trace of vulgar triumph, or to Emma the slightest shadow of meanness. Nor does Shaw allow our sympathies to get out of hand; indeed I have not heard him accused of ever doing so. His tolerance and fairness are admirable, and he always respects genuine feeling. He has the dramatist's enjoyment of all the varieties of human behaviour; he seems to love his characters for their foibles; but as I have said his comedy is concerned with the clash between points of view, and his characters are strictly *dramatis personae*—mouthpieces. I can think of no exception: even St Joan. Moreover, he holds the balance between points of view as skilfully as Jane Austen (or Chaucer, the supreme example) does between characters. If we regard him as a propagandist, we are constantly left wondering what side he is on. In *Major Barbara*, not on Undershaft's, nor on Barbara's, and certainly not on Cusins's. Even Mrs Baines (who is the least intelligent of the main characters in this scene, and in the weakest position) produces an unanswerable argument: 'Will there be less drinking or more if all these poor souls we are saving come tomorrow and find the doors of our shelter shut in their faces?'; and Barbara accepts her argument, and tells her she is right to take the money.

The common factor in these four passages is an artistic detachment which takes the form of balance or proportion. That is a clue to the quality and value of comedy. It is also a link between comedy and laughter; for laughter is the commonest expression of a sense of humour, and the sense of humour, though not identical with this kind of detachment, usually accompanies it. The particular value of comedy is that it is both comprehensive and precise in its response to life. Indeed, these two qualities are connected. To have a truly discriminating palate one needs a healthy digestion.

Comprehensiveness and precision of mind are not everything; man needs not only self-knowledge and knowledge of the world, but also the 'courage never to submit or yield'. So in literature comedy and tragedy are complementary, and both necessary. Tragedy is a bulwark of human self-respect against the superhuman or inhuman forces pressing upon us from all sides. Comedy is our corresponding weapon against the forces of disintegration within human society, and against the germs of anarchy and defeatism in our own minds.

3

SUBJECT MATTER

I

I began this book by saying that comedy depends on the eye of the beholder, not on the character of the object he has in view; that nothing in nature is categorically comic—whether it is so or not depends on what you make of it. It would seem to follow that anything or everything is suitable subject matter for comedy. From a strictly philosophical point of view, that is so. But comedy is a tradition as well as an idea; and to the writer and reader of comedy the selection of subject matter and setting is as important as abstract notions about art, if not more so. Of course, in making his selection, the writer will be influenced consciously or unconsciously by the ideal character of his art, or at least by his opinions about it.

He is trying to present a social point of view; to measure human conduct against a norm rather than an ideal. He is, or should be, actuated always by a sense of proportion. What he depicts—his subject matter—may therefore be defined as the abnormal. He may include some normal characters in his work, to serve as a kind of yard-stick; but for the most part he will leave his public to deduce his norm from the way he depicts the clash and contrast of varied abnormalities. In any case, far the greater part of his matter must inevitably be abnormal.

This indicates another difference between tragedy and comedy. It has been argued convincingly that the characters and even the events in a tragedy must be normal if we are to feel the full tragic effect. But can the character and behaviour of Macbeth, for example, be called normal? A clear distinction must be drawn between the *normal* and the *usual*. Tragedy of course deals with unusual situations and consequently with unusual states of mind; but we should always feel that the situation is one in which we might have been placed, and that in similar circumstances we should, or at least very probably might, have felt as the characters of the tragedy do. We should be able to identify ourselves with them for the time being. The problem for the tragic writer is to bridge the gap between the terrible and the normal: to show us, for example, a murderer like Macbeth or a madman like Lear, who yet retain the deepest and sanest human feelings. He does this, not by stressing normality, but by making us feel it as an undertone in the situation: by speeches like Macbeth's

> If thou couldst, doctor, cast
> The water of my land, find her disease,
> And purge it to a sound and pristine health,
> I would applaud thee to the very echo,
> That should applaud again;

or Lear's

> Poor naked wretches, wheresoe'er you are
> That bide the pelting of this pitiless storm,
> How shall your houseless heads and unfed sides,
> Your loop'd and window'd raggedness, defend you
> From seasons such as these?

It may be said that whereas tragedy deals with the unusual but normal, comedy deals with the abnormal but not unusual. The abnormality of comic characters is not absolute; we should feel that they are capable of behaving normally if they would. But it is the main concern of the comic writer to discriminate between what is normal and abnormal in human behaviour; he is detached from his subject matter in a sense in which other artists are not. He needs not merely a strong feeling for normality, but also a clear notion of it. It is therefore necessary for him to be in some measure a moral philosopher; for the norm is a philosophical concept. The usual, or average, is not; it can be calculated statistically from observed facts. But normality, like the cognate concepts of health and sanity, is not a fact, nor a complex of facts, nor even a simplification of facts; it is an idea, and exists only in the mind that has brought itself to bear on all the relevant facts. There is not one norm of human behaviour,

Subject matter

but many: some of them widely divergent and even contradictory. Jane Austen's norm differs drastically in some respects from Chaucer's or Fielding's. But all comic writers must have a norm in view. To detect eccentricity you must have a centre: that is to say a consistent, if not consciously worked out, standard of character and conduct.

From these considerations it might be deduced that the world of comedy would be a realistically depicted world peopled by eccentric characters. This formula fits some comic writers: Fielding and Jane Austen in particular. It was also the formula laid down by Ben Jonson and in the main followed by him. But as a general definition it is too narrow, and also radically misleading. Meredith puts his finger on the error contained in it, in the passage I have quoted on page 15: comedy *may be taken for* a slavish reflex of real life, *until its features are closely studied*. There is always an element of caricature in comedy, the caricature being so designed as to stress the eccentricity of the individual. Everyone, however nearly normal, has his foibles, however slight. But this, perhaps, is obvious.

A more serious objection to this formula is that comedy is not necessarily at all realistic in technique. None of Shakespeare's comedies are: even *Measure for Measure,* which is often classed as a realistic play, is strange and remote—suffused in 'the light that never was on sea or land'. The fable (as used by Aesop, for example) is one of the earliest and most efficient vehicles for comedy, and it is quite unrealistic. Even allegory, which is more unrealistic still, adapts itself well and easily to comic purposes: the vice in the late medieval morality plays was a comic figure, and probaby the literary ancestor of Shakespeare's Falstaff. Even in so tedious an allegory as the *Roman de la Rose* the character of Fals-Semblant is fully developed comedy; it provided Chaucer with the outline of the character of his Pardoner. Chaucer himself took his first exercises in comedy in *The House of Fame* and *The Parliament of Fowls* (an allegory and a fable). I have already called attention to the technique of the Bottom-Titania scene in *A Midsummer Night's Dream,* which is unrealistic and close to allegory. The best plays of the first great European comic writer, Aristophanes, are all fantasies, although the central character in an Aristophanic comedy is usually a realistically conceived middle-aged and middle-class Athenian citizen. There is a similar blend of realism and fantasy in the greatest of all European comedies, *Don Quixote*; and there is comedy, both realistic and unrealistic, in Bunyan's *Pilgrim's Progress*, the general structure of which is allegorical.

Even this cursory survey shows that comedy demands the utmost latitude in its choice of setting and in the form of its subject matter; and that its bias is away from rather than towards, a close imitation, or as Meredith puts it, a slavish reflexion, of real life.

II

In the prologue to *Everyman in his Humour*, Ben Jonson professed to 'sport with human follies, not with crimes'; and perhaps there is little more to be said about the subject matter of comedy. According to the gentler Congreve, natural folly (being incurable) is not a fit subject for comedy; it is unseemly to mock at it; he therefore took affectation for the theme of his masterpiece, *The Way of the World*. This seems on the whole to have been Shakespeare's practice also. It is a more attractive, and perhaps profounder, notion than Jonson's (though, by the way, affectation was one of the main follies Jonson ridiculed). But Congreve's scruples limit comedy rather too drastically. Even in *The Way of the World* one has to strain the definition of affectation to the utmost if it is to cover the criminal folly of Mrs Marwood and the criminal cunning of Fainall; though if duplicity may be regarded as a crude form of affectation the formula will work. There are advantages in Jonson's wider formula. He himself certainly did not regard folly as either natural or incurable. And if the stress is laid on folly, rather than wickedness on the one hand or misfortune on the other, it follows that the comic situation is involuntary but avoidable, whereas the tragic hero deliberately (if blindly) presses on to an inevitable doom. This is very generally true.

But Jonson's formula does not tell us very much. For one thing, folly can be tragic without being actually criminal, as in Lear, and perhaps also some of Shakespeare's other heroes. Further, both Jonson and Congreve seem to assume that comic situations arise solely from flaws in character. This is not so. They can arise between quite healthy people (like Higgins and Eliza in *Pygmalion*) as the result of natural or accidental misunderstanding, though unless they are to be merely farcical, character must play a part in them. The situation need not be caused by character, but it must reveal character. Perhaps the subject matter of comedy might be defined as 'curable or manageable faults or maladjustments'. The disturbances with which comedy deals are not always curable; but if they cannot be cured, then their ill-effects are strictly circumscribed; they do not ultimately cause widespread damage to the society in which they occur, and when they are finally isolated in the lives of one or two people, they do not prevent even those people from finding a *modus vivendi*. The situation in Molière's *Misantrope* is of that kind. On the other hand, where the disturbance leads to or results from the widespread maladjustments of a whole group of people, it must be such as to work itself out to a cure. That would describe the situation in *Tom Jones*.

Is comedy then essentially trivial? In one sense, yes.

> Great things are done when men and mountains meet;
> This is not done by jostling in the street.

These two lines of Blake's are good symbols for tragedy and comedy. But what happens as we jostle against each other in our homes and businesses and villages and towns is perhaps by accumulation more important than the 'great things' in determining human happiness and unhappiness, and even in determining the way of the world.

It is not therefore surprising that easily the favourite topic of comedy is sex. In no other department of life is there more 'jostling'. And nowhere else can we *all* be said to be eccentric; but here we can. All women appear abnormal to all men, and all men abnormal to all women; and rightly, for sex carries with it specialisation and so a departure from the *common* human pattern. This departure is accentuated in civilised life. There is a wide gap between the impulses that precede and accompany human mating, and the codes of manners and sentiment between men and women that prevail from time to time. Such widely different works as Chaucer's *Troilus and Criseyde*, Fielding's *Tom Jones*, and Shaw's *Candida*, all make comedy out of the clash between sentiment and behaviour, the ideal and the real. It is this inconsistency in almost all civilisations and almost all people that makes the comic writers choose sex for one of their main themes, and also makes comedy the best, perhaps the only really humane, attitude to sex. For comedy denies neither the romance and delicacy that has in some odd way become a second nature in civilised men and women, nor the primitive chase, enticement, conquest, and yielding that we share with other animals.

And lastly the mere fact that no other human relationship is so natural as this one; that the survival of the race depends on it; and that it is the commonest disturbing influence to which human nature and social life are subject—this ensures that it should be the most persistent theme of comedy.

And so, in fact, it is: in Chaucer and Shakespeare, in Restoration Comedy, in Fielding and Sterne, Sheridan and Goldsmith, Jane Austen and Bernard Shaw.

But, alas, comedy has given the most widespread and bitter offence by its attitude to sex. It seems that whatever the comic writer does someone will complain loudly. Jane Austen writes within the strictest bounds of propriety; so she is charged with prudishness. She has her 'centre' from which to judge what is or is not socially normal; and from it she utterly condemns all licence between men and women. Moreover, as an artist, she 'quits such odious subjects as soon as she can'. I do not think that even the fanatics of literary criticism insist that she ought to *approve* of licentiousness; but they do complain that she leaves the unruly workings of passion out of her books. It may be replied to this complaint that she is under no obligation to depict erotic passion; but that if it could be proved that she ignores it or pretends that it does not exist, she might be charged with prudishness. It cannot be proved; and the contrary can be proved. It is the impact of Lydia's seduction on *Pride and Prejudice* that shocks the characters of the story out of their unreally trivial life. In *Mansfield Park* loose conduct is analysed (though not depicted) in some detail in the characters of Henry and Mary Crawford, who are condemned not for the strength of their passions, but for shallowness and lack of sensibility. The main theme of *Persuasion* is the danger of allowing one's feelings to be swayed overmuch by prudence and the worldly advice of one's seniors. And let those who think that Jane Austen handles sex timidly, read this passage from *Sanditon*:

> Sir Edward's great object in life was to be seductive. With such personal advantages as he knew himself to possess, and such talents as he did also give himself credit for, he regarded it as his duty. He felt that he was formed to be a dangerous man—quite in the line of the Lovelaces.

Subject matter 47

The very name of Sir Edward, he thought, carried some degree of fascination with it. To be generally gallant and assiduous about the fair, to make fine speeches to every pretty girl, was but the inferior part of the character he had to play. Miss Heywood, or any other young woman with any pretensions to beauty, he was entitled (according to his own views of Society) to approach with high compliment and rhapsody on the slightest acquaintance; but it was Clara alone on whom he had serious designs; it was Clara whom he meant to seduce. Her seduction was quite determined on. Her situation in every way called for it. She was his rival in Lady Denham's favour, she was young, lovely and dependent. He had very early seen the necessity of the case, and had now been long trying with cautious assiduity, to make an impression on her heart, and to undermine her principles. Clara saw through him, and had not the least intention of being seduced; but she bore with him patiently enough to confirm the sort of attachment which her personal charms had raised. A greater degree of discouragement, indeed, would not have affected Sir Edward. He was armed against the highest pitch of disdain or aversion. If she could not be won by affection, he must carry her off. He knew his business. Already had he had many musings on the subject. If he *were* constrained so to act, he must naturally wish to strike out something new, to exceed those who had gone before him; and he felt a strong curiosity to ascertain whether the neighbourhood of Timbuctoo might not afford some solitary house adapted to Clara's reception; but the expense, alas! of measures in that masterly style was ill-suited to his purse, and prudence obliged him to prefer the quietest sort of ruin and disgrace for the object of his affections to the more renowned.

It is not however by squeamishness that comedy most often gives offence, but by licentiousness or obscenity. The two charges are usually confused or combined, but they are really quite different; it is one thing to advocate lax conduct, and quite a different thing to display in the open matters over which politeness draws a veil. The former concerns morality; the latter good taste. Let us therefore treat the first as a moral question and the second as an aesthetic question.

In its historical beginnings comedy was a species of authorised licence. That does not mean that it was an attack on morality, good manners, or social discipline; in fact, Aristophanes (the only dramatist of this phase whose works have survived in bulk) had and expressed strict views about conduct, and in the *Frogs* he takes Euripides to task for laxity of principle about many matters, including sex. Aristophanes is far from primitive in his dramatic art, indeed he was the very last writer of the Attic Old Comedy; but his plays belong to the licentious class. What this means is that the comedy was a safety-valve or outlet for disorderly passions, including erotic passions; and by treating them in an unserious spirit it rendered them less dangerous socially. How far this has remained a deliberate purpose of comic writers is very doubtful. It seems to have been in Fielding's mind when he wrote *Tom Jones*; Tom's frequent falls from grace are upon the whole treated as a joke, for two reasons. Fielding does not wish to approve of them, but at the same time he wishes to insist that natural faults are curable, and far less serious than cold-blooded selfish dishonesty, as exemplified in Tom's foil, Blifil. I think almost any scene in *Tom Jones* makes Fielding's attitude clear; this passage from chapter 10 of the Fifth Book will do as well as any:

Jones retired from the company in which we have seen him engaged, into the fields, where he intended to cool himself by a walk in the open air before he attended Mr Allworthy. There, whilst he renewed those meditations on his dear Sophia which the dangerous illness of his friend and benefactor had for some time interrupted, an accident happened, which with sorrow we relate, and with sorrow, doubtless, will it be read; however, that historic truth to which we profess so inviolable an attachment obliges us to communicate it to posterity.

It was now a pleasant evening in the latter end of June, when our hero was walking in a most delicious grove, where the gentle breezes fanning the leaves, together with the sweet trilling of a murmuring stream, and the melodious notes of nightingales, formed all together the most enchanting harmony. In this scene, so sweetly accommodated to love, he meditated on his dear Sophia. While his wanton fancy roved unbounded over all her beauties, and his lively imagination painted the charming maid in various ravishing forms, his warm heart melted with tenderness, and at length, throwing himself on the ground by the side of a gently murmuring brook, he broke forth into the following ejaculation:

'O Sophia, would Heaven give thee to my arms, how blest would be my condition! Curst be that fortune which sets a distance between us! Was I but possessed of thee, one only suit of rags thy whole estate, is there a man on earth whom I would envy? How contemptible would the brightest Circassian beauty, drest in all the jewels of the Indies, appear to my eyes! But why do I mention another woman? Could I think my eyes capable of looking at any other with tenderness, these hands should tear them from my head. No, my Sophia, if cruel fortune separates us for ever, my soul shall doat on thee alone. The chastest constancy will I ever preserve to thy image. Though I should never have possession of thy charming person, still shalt thou alone have possession of my thoughts, my love, my soul. Oh! my fond heart is so wrapt in that tender bosom, that the brightest beauties would for me have no charms, nor would a hermit be colder in their embraces. Sophia, Sophia alone, shall be mine. What raptures are in that name! I will engrave it on every tree.'

At these words he started up, and beheld—not his Sophia—no, nor a Circassian maid richly and elegantly attired for the grand signior's seraglio. No; without a gown, in a shift that was somewhat of the coarsest and none of the cleanest, bedewed likewise with some odoriferous effluvia, the produce of the day's labour, with a pitchfork in her hand, Molly Seagrim approached. Our hero had his penknife in his hand, which he had drawn for the before-mentioned purpose of carving on the bark; when the girl, coming near him, cried out with a smile, 'You don't intend to kill me, squire, I hope?' 'Why should you think I would kill you?' answered Jones. 'Nay,' replied she, 'after your cruel usage of me when I saw you last, killing me would, perhaps, be too great kindness for me to expect.'

Here ensued a parley, which, as I do not think myself obliged to relate, I shall omit. It is sufficient that it lasted a full quarter of an hour, at the conclusion of which they retired into the thickest part of the grove.

But in other writers, such as Chaucer, there seems no such motive, or if it is present it is very slight. The 'swiving' of the Miller's wife and daughter in the *Reeve's Tale* is described with the most lighthearted high spirits; for the girl it was perhaps a piece of pleasure and kindness that had rarely come her way in a home presided over by such unpleasant parents (Chaucer may not have meant to imply this, but he certainly implies that she enjoyed her night with the young man); for the parents it was a comic punishment of their self-importance and of the miller's dishonesty. In *Troilus and Criseyde*, the detailed description of Criseyde's seduction, and particularly Pandarus's part in it, serves a different purpose. Partly it brings out a contrast between the characters of Pandarus and Criseyde on the one hand and Troilus on the other; and partly it reveals the divided impulses in Troilus himself, for the main theme of the poem is the inconsistency of feeling and motive in which he is involved (like all decent and natural young lovers) between plain physical desire and respect for the feelings and interests of the woman. The convention of courtly love was one of those codes of sentiment for civilising sex of which I have spoken; it is not to be despised, nor does Chaucer despise it; the despairs and scruples of

Troilus are by no means unnatural and have their counterpart even in enlightened (or cynical) ages like the present. But love is desire as well as sentiment; Chaucer's Troilus was a flesh-and-blood young man, not a mere collection of ideals; he wanted to possess Criseyde and he was human enough to enjoy possessing her. The truth to life of this great love story demanded that every side of Criseyde's seduction should be fully revealed. Yet although Chaucer included *Troilus and Criseyde* among the sinful works of which he repented in his famous retraction at the end of the *Canterbury Tales*, it is not in the least an immoral work. The love-affair comes to grief because of faults in all the three main characters; but chiefly because Pandarus, by his well-meaning but unprincipled interference, degraded it into a mere fornication.

But there are comic works that are more reasonably accused of advocating licence. All our Restoration comedies, from Etherege to Farquhar, take seduction for granted as a normal form of sport, which indeed upon the whole it was for Charles II and his courtiers. The mere fact that they take it *for granted* partially acquits them of advocating it; and Wycherley, who has the worst reputation of them all, was obviously unhappy about its results and implications —so much so that *The Country Wife*, in which he accepts it and exploits its comic possibilities without reserve, is a far healthier and therefore more moral play than *The Plain Dealer*, in which he is both fiercely satirical and morbidly sentimental. *The Country Wife*, indeed, has a moral, and a sound one: that the husband who mistrusts his wife and tries to keep her from other men will merely stimulate her desires and teach her to deceive him, however ill-equipped she is with natural cunning. This is in accord with the rationalism of the period. The comic dramatists of the late seventeenth century treat sex as an opportunity for pleasure but a potential source of trouble; and their norm of conduct is to get a fair share of the pleasure with the least possible distress to all concerned. For the most part their men and women are of the same class, and treat each other as equals; and in one respect their morality compares favourably with the average Victorian morality, for they have roughly the same standards for men as for women. The Victorian code (both legal and social) was that whereas a wife should forgive her husband's infidelity if he asked her to, a husband was under no obligation to forgive his wife's. In the seventeenth century, divorce could only be obtained by an *ad hoc* Act of Parliament; it

Subject matter

was therefore very rare, and perhaps for that very reason there was greater mutual tolerance among civilised people, though of course they were often very unhappy, as is made clear by Halifax's *Advice to a Daughter*. And there were husbands who literally locked their wives up, though public opinion censured that kind of behaviour. A cynic might say that there was an obvious reason for the censure: that every man was interested in having his neighbour's wife at large and accessible. But the cynicism would not be altogether justified; cynicism seldom is. The Restoration wits, however little respect they had for the Seventh Commandment, were upon the whole humane towards women and respected them as equals. There were among them notorious rakes, such as Rochester; but the general feeling was against the extremes of debauchery. That is at any rate the standpoint of Etherege, Congreve and Vanbrugh. Wycherley's Horner is not a typical Restoration gentleman; he is a comic rogue, comparable on a different plane to Shakespeare's Autolycus or Ben Jonson's Volpone; his function is to expose the other characters and keep the plot in motion.

But for the moralist to condemn any comedy because of its subject matter is an error of judgment. It is not the business of comedy to inculcate moral doctrine. Its business is to satisfy a healthy human desire; the desire to understand the behaviour of men and women towards one another in social life, and to judge them according to their own pretensions and standards. So far as it does this well and truly it makes for righteousness. We may, and probably most of us do, dissent from the moral standards of Etherege or Wycherley, at least in part; but unless our morality is of the kind that needs wrapping up in cotton wool, we need not be protected against their plays. I will go further than this: even assuming that the moral standards of Restoration Comedy are utterly bad, we ought to be able to enjoy the comedies themselves, and to do so will strengthen rather than weaken our moral fibre, provided always that we have grown out of the cotton wool stage. All we are justified in asking of the comic writer is that his standards should be consistent; not that they should be right. The whole question is part of a wider quarrel between moralists and artists. But let me make it clear that I am not on the side of the artist *against* the moralist; I believe myself to be on the side of morality *and* art, as Milton was in *Areopagitica* and Shelley in his *Defence of Poetry*.

With the other charge, of obscenity, as it is much less serious, I will be very brief. There are people who object to many comedies, and particularly all Restoration comedies on the ground that they are indecent. It is difficult, and perhaps futile, to argue about questions of taste such as this. We can only state our own tastes and plead for some tolerance on both sides of the question. Sex is a nuisance; we all sometimes wish we could dispense with it. But there it is; and just as the poets have paid tribute to its noblest and most beautiful manifestations and also reviled it for cruelties and humiliations, so let the comic writers enjoy it as the greatest of eternal jokes. But let them do it with a certain discretion of speech. I cannot see the objection to innuendo. It offends some people, who feel it to be cowardly; if we are to have filth, they say, let us have frank filth. But this use of the word filth is equivocal; and it is begging the question to equate coarseness with frankness. In literature and drama, surely the crude and limited vocabulary of the navvy and that of the clinical lecture-room are equally out of place —and they are the only two perfectly plain vocabularies available for use in this connexion. It is true that the point of an innuendo can be missed, if one is not on the look-out; but on this, of all subjects, it is proper to make jokes with a certain finesse.

The most daring and notorious joke in Restoration Comedy occurs in Act IV, scene iii of *The Country Wife*, where Wycherley comes as near as possible to depicting 'the lineaments of gratified' (and ungratified) 'desire' by a very clever innuendo.

[*Re-enter Lady Fidget with a piece of china in her hand, and Horner following.*]
LADY FIDGET [*to Mrs Squeamish*] ... I have been toiling and moiling, for the prettiest piece of china, my dear.
HORNER Nay, she has been too hard for me, do what I could.
MRS SQUEAMISH Oh lord, I'll have some china too. Good Mr Horner, don't think to give other people china, and me none; come in with me too.
HORNER Upon my honour, I have none left now.
MRS SQUEAMISH Nay, nay, I have known you deny your china before now, but you shan't put me off so, come——
HORNER This lady had the last there.
LADY FIDGET Yes, indeed, Madam, to my certain knowledge, he has no more left.
MRS SQUEAMISH O, but it may be he may have some you could not find.
LADY FIDGET What, d'ye think if he had had any left, I would not have had it too? for we women of quality never think we have china enough.

Subject matter

HORNER Do not take it ill I cannot make china for you all; but I will have a roll-wagon for you too, another time.
MRS SQUEAMISH Thank you, dear toad.

The disguise is purely verbal and scenic; there can be no doubt of what the characters are talking about. The question, and it is merely a question of taste, is whether it should be talked about so openly on the stage. The answer will depend mainly on whether the situation is comic, or only coarse; and comic it certainly is in this scene. But anyone who is squeamish had better not go to see *The Country Wife* without first reading it.

III

Comedy depicts men and women in society. Meredith stresses this point; and it leads him to the questionable conclusion that the setting of comedy should be urban and that Shakespeare's characters, being 'creatures of the woods and wilds' are 'subjects of a special study in the poetically comic'. It is true that Shakespeare's comedy is unique, because of his apparent inability to write with his imagination at less than full stretch: he was *incapable* of realism. But it is not clear, without better reasons than Meredith gives, that pure comedy cannot be staged in a fairy-tale setting as successfully as in Paris or London. Meredith seems to have been misled by the special narrow use of the word society in the Victorian and Edwardian periods, and indeed to have been obsessed by the idea of Society with a capital S: a select class of wealthy and leisured persons, speaking an artificial language of their own and spending all their time and energy in entertaining themselves and one another. Certainly that kind of society provides a good setting for comedy; but to *limit* comedy to it is simply to fly in the face of the facts.

Characters like Bottom were too close to nature for Meredith's strict notion of comedy; and Titania, a 'creature of the woods and wilds', was quite outside his pale. But no particular class of person or environment is in itself either comic or un-comic; it is the imagination of the writer or spectator that makes them so. Meredith's argument is parallel to the orthodox renascence convention of dramatic propriety, according to which a king or a statesman should not be made ridiculous or contemptible. Dr Johnson met this pedantry with a common sense if not completely conclusive rejoinder:

> Shakespeare always makes nature predominate over accident; and if he preserves the essential character, is not very careful of distinctions superinduced and adventitious. His story requires Romans or Kings, but he thinks only on men. He knew that Rome, like any other city, had men of all dispositions; and wanting a buffoon he went into the Senate-house for that which the Senate-house would certainly have afforded him. He was inclined to shew an usurper and a murderer not only odious but despicable, he therefore added drunkenness to his other qualities, knowing that kings love wine like other men, and that wine exerts its natural power upon kings. These are the petty cavils of petty minds; a poet overlooks the casual distinctions of country and condition, as a painter, satisfied with the figure, neglects the drapery.

As for Meredith's thesis, it is probably true that man in his urban environment lends himself more readily to comedy; and certainly true that comedy is essentially concerned with men and not with fairies. But all art is in greater or less degree symbolic: as Johnson said, imitations convince not because they are mistaken for realities, but because they bring realities to mind. Surely even in the strictest sense, rustics can be comic, and not only rustics but animals and even vegetables; and not only things in nature, but purely imaginary creatures like Titania. In transporting Bottom into fairy-land Shakespeare knew very well what he was doing, and was well within his rights as a comic dramatist. The situation of course is unrealistic and dreamlike; but anyone who has himself dreamed will know how much richer in comedy the world of dreams is than the circumspect world of every-day working reality.

Society in the proper sense—or at least in the sense in which the word defines the setting of comedy—stands for an idea rather than a particular set of persons. It stands for coherence; for a common body of opinions and standards and a disposition to co-operate. It can be contracted to a very small class living together in a small area; it can be extended to the whole of humanity or even beyond the limits of the human species. Its extent will depend partly on the power of statesmen, philosophers, and artists to impose unity on apparently heterogeneous material; partly on the social conditions of the time and place in which they are living; partly on the purpose they have in view. To the mind of Shakespeare and his fellow-

Subject matter

Elizabethans the universe was more homogeneous than it is to us; for our moral ideas lag behind the lessons of modern physics and economics. Shakespeare did not therefore need to restrict his setting at all. The distinctions between man, beast, and spirit, which our minds can only surmount by a change of gear and often a very violent one, did not trouble him; Prospero, Ariel, and Caliban are all members of one society. For Chaucer it was the same. His range was somewhat narrower; but that was because his imagination, powerful and adventurous though it was, had not quite the range of Shakespeare's, not because the medieval world was in any except the strictly material sense narrower than the Elizabethan. Chaucer's comic world contains Chantecleer, and the Eagle in the *House of Fame*; January and May in the *Merchant's Tale* (the story is an allegory, though a very realistic one); the Prioress and the Wife of Bath; Troilus, Criseyde, and Pandarus. It is a world at least as varied, if not quite so cosmic, as Shakespeare's.

But about the beginning of the Seventeenth Century the outlook of the educated Englishman changed; not in a single generation, but with the rapidity of a revolution. Men's eyes turned towards the material world in which they lived; and in this movement towards materialistic rationalism Ben Jonson was the central literary figure, as he was also the founder of modern comedy. There were to be no more fairies in comedy. Into the merits of the controversy about realism I will not go here. One can only be thankful that Jonson was in the field a few years later than Shakespeare, and not a few years earlier. But probably the reaction was both inevitable and salutary. Fletcher's realistic comedies are altogether superior to *The Faithful Shepherdess* and the romantic tragedies and tragicomedies that earned him from Dryden the disparaging description, 'a limb of Shakespeare'. Be this as it may, Jonson narrowed the field to particular time and place. But his own comedy was still very wide in range. Society for him was still at least as wide as human nature, though his imagination was only at its ease in the underworld of London. The test his characters have to submit to—the standard they have to satisfy—is a hard but crude one. They have to survive in the world of *Bartholomew Fair*.

Later writers, lacking the large ideal vision of Shakespeare and Chaucer, and the robust digestion of Jonson, have discovered an excellent convention which is sometimes called the Comic Microcosm. They take for the setting of their comedy a 'little world', a strictly limited society with fairly homogeneous traditions, standards, and habits. In such a world, where the rules of the game of life are the same for everybody, where all know the rules and accept them in theory at least, it is easy to measure men and women against each other fairly, and to pick out the good and the bad mixers, at the same time depicting even in the good mixers those faults of temperament and foibles of the intellect that cause both the graver irritations and the pleasant smaller frictions provocative of nothing worse than a smile. The first very clear example of the Comic Microcosm in our literature is the world of Restoration comedy. Perhaps Etherege, the earliest of the Restoration comic dramatists, deserves the credit of discovering it; but he did not invent it, he saw it around him. How closely he followed in his plays the pattern of a real little world in which he lived may be seen from his letters. I have said something of the standards of this society, and it only remains to repeat that for the purpose of comedy (as outlined in the third sentence of this paragraph) it does not matter so much that they should be morally sound as that they should be consistent, clearly understood, and generally accepted within the society.

The world of Restoration comedy, small and never very important historically, soon melted away. In the eighteenth century English civilisation broke up into innumerable units centred in the home. This decentralisation gave birth to *The Spectator*; and Addison created around Sir Roger de Coverley a kind of domestic comedy new to English literature, unless it had been foreshadowed by the country seat of Mr Justice Shallow in Shakespeare's *Henry IV*. In a nation alive with vigorous and self-centred homes the domestic world offers an obvious microcosm to the comic writer. In the early days of our literature, Chaucer had used it for many of his best Canterbury Tales. In eighteenth-century England domestic comedy revived. By a charming irony it was a homeless Irish wanderer, Goldsmith, who wrote the best of all our domestic plays, *She Stoops to Conquer*; I wish I could rank his even more domestic novel *The Vicar of Wakefield* as highly, but it is too unequal, ill-constructed, and heterogeneous to be quite successful as a comedy or anything else. I suppose the most *remarkable* of all domestic microcosms is Shandy Hall, the setting of one of the greatest and most sustained flights of comic imagination in our literature. But a single home is rather small to allow comedy to display its full powers; *Tristram Shandy* is a tour-de-force, and Sterne himself is

Subject matter

rather too much of a virtuoso—even an exhibitionist—to keep consistently within the bounds of comedy. Jane Austen saw what was wanted; her 'three or four families in a country village' provided the most successful, and famous, of all English comic microcosms.

No later writer has created comedy to equal hers. Trollope's Barsetshire is a convincing little world and offers some high moments of comedy: the death of Mrs Proudie, for instance. Unfortunately it is not a purely *comic* microcosm; Trollope sacrifices too many of his characters to the demons of sensationalism and sentimentality. Meredith's 'Society' is too unreal to serve convincingly as a measure of character. Shaw did not choose to use any consistent convention for his settings; they are varied, and all of them more or less fantastic even when they appear most realistic. Since his comedy is a comedy of ideas its material setting has little importance except for theatrical purposes. He has a sort of intellectual microcosm: the world of self-conscious middle-class ideas which flourished at the end of the nineteenth century. One is conscious in his plays of a consistent *milieu*, in which the mental habits of his characters can be accurately measured against each other. Lastly, James Joyce's Dublin is a little world within which he achieved a masterpiece; but *Ulysses* is more than a comedy, it is what he intended it to be, an epic.

4

STYLE

It is in the style of a play or novel that we first recognise comedy; and that is probably a surer touchstone than any theory. To say this is not to give more weight to style in comedy than in other forms of art; the proposition that style *is* art would not be far wide of the mark. But since its subject matter tends towards the commonplace, comedy is bound to rely mainly on style for producing its generic effect. Everyone knows how a talented story-teller can make a quite pointless anecdote comic by his tone, expression, and gesture; and how easy it is to spoil a good story by neglecting these accompaniments. The comic writer has to put his work into a form which will make it as difficult as possible for anyone to spoil it in the reading. A dramatist may hope for help from his actors; if he is lucky, they may correct deficiencies in his art, but he would be unwise to rely on that, and wise to safeguard himself against the risk that they will spoil rather than enhance it. That Congreve had a great actress to play the parts of his heroines no doubt helped him; we can never know how much the accent (or for the matter of that the whole character) of Millamant owes to Mrs Bracegirdle. The knowledge that he could rely on her support and talent must have given Congreve confidence and stimulus; probably her stage personality served as a model for the speaking voices of all his heroines, for they have a family likeness. But for his posthumous reputation a dramatist has to rely on the written dialogue he leaves behind him; and even at a first performance he is fortunate if he has any considerable say in what the producer and the actors do with his words. Congreve's plays are alive today because his dialogue is

Style

imperishable; even if his present popularity owes something to Sir Nigel Playfair and Dame Edith Evans.

Tragedy has its characteristic accent too. The most striking and lasting effect of Shakespeare's tragedies comes from the poetry; for instance, from the soliloquies of Hamlet and Macbeth, or speeches like Othello's

> 'Soft you; a word or two before you go . . .'

This accent marks not only the dialogue of tragic drama but also the narrative parts of the tragic novel; as in these paragraphs from *The Mayor of Casterbridge*:

> Henchard's lips half parted to begin an explanation. But he shut them up like a vice, and uttered not a sound. How should he, there and then, set before her with any effect the palliatives of his great faults—that he had himself been deceived in her identity at first, till informed by her mother's letter that her own child had died; that, in the second accusation, his lie had been the last desperate throw of a gamester who loved her affection better than his own honour? Among the many hindrances to such a pleading not the least was this, that he did not sufficiently value himself to lessen his sufferings by strenuous appeal or elaborate argument.
>
> Waiving, therefore, his privilege of self-defence, he regarded only her discomposure. 'Don't ye distress yourself on my account,' he said, with proud superiority. 'I would not wish it—at such a time, too, as this. I have done wrong in coming to 'ee—I see my error. But it is only for once, so forgive it. I'll never trouble 'ee again, Elizabeth-Jane—no, not to my dying day! Good night! Good-bye!'
>
> Then, before she could collect her thoughts, Henchard went out from her rooms, and departed from the house by the back way as he had come; and she saw him no more.

I do not mean to say that given any similar passage, out of its context, an experienced reader would at once with certainty pronounce 'This comes from a tragedy'. To suppose that literature has such a sort of uniformity is unscientific; just as it is unscientific to jump to conclusions about a man's character from a single isolated action or remark, however revealing it may appear to be. There are varieties of tragic style; and inevitably many parts even of the great tragedies of Shakespeare are pitched in a lower or different key. But it is by this high and grave tone, however intermittent, that we most surely feel the quality, and recognise the character, of tragedy.

Comedy has to be distinguished not only from tragedy but also —more difficult—from satire and farce; as well as from other ways of writing that are neither tragedy nor comedy, nor anything in particular. It has its characteristic imagery, as in this speech of Millamant in *The Way of the World*:

> Sententious Mirabell! Prithee don't look with that violent and inflexible wise Face, like Solomon at the dividing of the Child in an old Tapestry Hanging,—

its characteristic rhythm:

> LADY PLIANT Nay, nay, rise up, come you shall see my good Nature. I know Love is powerful, and nobody can help his Passion: 'tis not your Fault; nor I swear it is not mine,—how can I help it, if I have Charms? And how can you help it, if you are made a Captive? I swear it is pity it should be a Fault,—But my Honour,—well, but your Honour too—but the Sin!—well, but the Necessity—O Lord, here's somebody coming, I dare not stay. Well, you must consider of your Crime; and strive as much as can be against it,—strive be sure—But don't be melancholic; don't despair,—But never think that I'll grant you anything; O Lord, no; —But be sure you lay aside all Thoughts of the Marriage, for tho' I know you don't love Cynthia, only as a blind for your Passion to me; yet it will make me jealous,—O Lord, what did I say? Jealous! no, no, I can't be jealous, for I must not love you,—therefore don't hope,—But don't despair neither,—O, they're coming, I must fly.

and its characteristic tone in telling a story:

> Mrs Morland was a very good woman, and wished to see her children everything they ought to be; but her time was so much occupied in lying-in and teaching the little ones, that her elder daughters were inevitably left to shift for themselves; and it was not very wonderful that Catherine, who had by nature nothing heroic about her, should prefer cricket, baseball, riding on horseback, and running about the country, at the age of fourteen, to books—or at least books of information—for, provided that nothing like useful knowledge could be gained from them, provided they were all story and no reflection, she had never any objection to books at all. But from fifteen to seventeen she was in training for a heroine; she read all such works as heroines must read to supply their memories with those quotations which are so serviceable and so soothing in the vicissitudes of their eventful lives.

But there is not one uniform style for comedy, any more than for tragedy. In the comic novel there is a particular reason for this, which does not apply to the tragic novel, or not to the same extent. As the comic writer is more detached from his characters (compare the two passages I have just quoted from *The Mayor of Casterbridge* and *Northanger Abbey*), so his narrative style will tend to differentiate itself more from the dialogue. And the better the artist, the more clearly it will do so. Neither Sterne nor Jane Austen, so far as I can remember, ever allowed the philosophical or judicial style they used for narration or comment to overflow into the dialogue in such a way as to make it lifeless or unconvincing. It is not necessary, even for a novelist, to reproduce the exact character of real-life talk; but he must vary the accents of his characters from his own, and from one another's, or they will not do for him the work they should.

The first requisite of a comic narrative is that it should be precise; the finest shades of character should stand revealed, and the situation must be clear. Chaucer's description of the first meeting of Troilus and Criseyde is a good example of that kind of precision. The scene takes place in a 'temple', which we may picture as a medieval church—I shall call it so. Criseyde is in church with the other people; everyone who sees her in her widow's weeds is delighted with her beauty—

> And yet she stood ful lowe and stille allone,
> Bihinden other folk, in litel brede,
> And neigh the dore, ay under shames drede,
> Simple of atir and debonaire of chere,
> With ful assured lokyng and manere.
>
> This Troilus, as he was wont to gide
> His yonge knyghtes, led hem up and down
> In thilke large temple on every side,
> Biholding ay the ladies of the town,
> Now here, now there; for no devocioun
> Hadde he to non, to reven him his reste,
> But gan to preise and lakken whom his leste.

This behaviour (as though he were a casual visitor to a cattle-show) would not even by our standards be good manners; by the medieval standard it was atrocious. But not only is his own attitude to the women insolent; he also watches his companions and takes it upon him to admonish any of them who show signs of a sentimental interest in any woman in the church. Troilus is clearly ripe for a lesson, and Chaucer interrupts his story with several stanzas of moralising. This is a regular habit of our older comic writers—it survived in force up to the time of Fielding and Sterne. The severer modern aesthetic theory frowns on it; we think, upon the whole, that the reader of a story should do his own moralising, while the writer contents himself with providing the data. This is no doubt sound theory; but there is loss as well as gain in the modern fear of being didactic. All our best comic writers do in fact moralise, though some less than others; and it would not be surprising if the older manner were to revive. There is more in comedy than the pleasures of cynicism, and the art might benefit if the writer made his own standards clearer by stating them directly. But it will suffice to quote one stanza only of Chaucer's moralising on this occasion.

> O blynde world, O blynde entencioun!
> How often falleth al the effect contraire
> Of surquidrie and foul presumpcioun;
> For caught is proud, and caught is debonaire.
> This Troilus is clomben on the staire,
> And litel weneth that he moot descenden;
> But alday faileth thing that fooles wenden.

Then his wandering eye falls on Criseyde, and there it comes to rest.

> And sodeynly he wax therwith astoned,
> And gan her bet biholde in thrifty wise.
> 'O mercy, God,' thoughte he, 'wher hastow woned
> That art so fair and goodly to devise?'
> Therwith his herte gan to sprede and rise,
> And softe sighed, lest men mighte him here
> And caught ayeyn his firste pleyinge chere.

Then follows a very exact description of Criseyde's appearance and of the behaviour of both of them.

> She nas nat with the leste of hir stature,
> But alle hir limmes so wel answerynge
> Weren to wommanhod, that creature
> Was nevere lesse mannysh in semynge.

And eek the pure wise of hir moevynge
Shewed wel that men myght in hire gesse
Honour, estat, and wommanly noblesse.

To Troilus right wonder wel with alle
Gan for to like hire moevynge and hire chere,
Which somdel deignous was, for she let falle
Hire look a lite aside in swich manere
Ascaunces, 'What! may I nat stonden here?'
And after that hir lookynge gan she lighte,
That nevere thoughte him seen so good a sighte.

And of hire look in him ther gan to quiken
So gret desir and swich affeccioun
That in his hertes botme gan to stiken
Of hir his fixe and depe impressioun.
And thogh he erst hadde poured up and doun,
He was tho glad his hornes in to shrinke;
Unnethes wiste he how to loke or winke.

Lo, he that leet himselven so connynge,
And scorned hem that Loves paynes dryen,
Was ful unwar that Love hadde his dwellynge
Withinne the subtile stremes of hir yen;
That sodeynly him thoughte he felte dyen
Right with hire look, the spirit in his herte.
Blissed be Love, that can thus folk converte!

She, this in blak, likynge to Troilus
Over alle thing, he stood for to biholde;
Ne his desir, ne wherfore he stood thus,
He neither chere made, ne word tolde;
But from afer, his manere for to holde,
On other thing his look som tyme he caste,
And eft on hire, while that the servyse laste.

And after this, nat fullich al awhaped,
Out of the temple al esilich he wente,
Repentynge him that he hadde evere yjaped
Of Loves folk, lest fully the descente
Of scorn felle on himself; but what he mente,
Lest it were wist on any manere side,
His woo he gan dissimulen and hide.

Chaucer is distinguished among comic writers by the attention he pays to the physical appearance of his characters; the descriptions in the Prologue to the *Canterbury Tales* are famous. He also believed that the attire proclaims the man, and particularly the woman. In this passage there is a general description of Criseyde's figure and deportment, a tableau of her appearance as she stood by the church door, and a motion picture of her behaviour when she caught Troilus's eye. Chaucer does not describe her dress in detail—it is black and simple; but he underlines it with a simile. Her beauty shone like a bright star under a black cloud. This is the second time in the poem Chaucer has shown her to us. We first see her going to Hector in private to enlist his soft heart, and his unequalled authority, for her protection. For that purpose she dressed in brown, a richer and warmer (but equally correct) colour; and her demeanour was far from 'assured'. In both scenes her stage-management is excellent, and has its immediate reward; she attends with care and skill to toilet, gesture, and expression, and also most scrupulously to the proprieties demanded by the occasion. The first time (in private) she is decidedly melodramatic, and Hector falls for her at once. The second time her mixture of self-effacement and assurance fascinates everyone who sees her. Thus in two complementary scenes Chaucer shows us what manner of woman she was by the description of externals alone; the most he *says* is that it was easy to guess that she was a respectable woman of position and good breeding.

He does not in this scene describe the appearance of Troilus. It is not important; Chaucer knows what to leave out as well as what to put in, as Dryden observed. But he tells us a great deal about his manner and behaviour. Troilus struts through the church like a proud peacock (the simile is Chaucer's), appraising the looks of the women. When he sees Criseyde, he is a lost man; but he puts up a fight at least so far as to save appearances for the time being. His tongue and expression are under control. He keeps his distance, and does not stare but steals glances. He is not quite out of his wits; when the service is over he manages to walk quietly out of church, and keeps up his banter of young men in love, though he sees it all too clearly recoiling on him, and repents of ever having begun it.

No other English writer can compete with Chaucer in descriptive skill except perhaps Sterne. The reader may turn back to page 24, where in a scene consisting almost entirely of dialogue the visible appearance and manner of the characters is nevertheless made most

Style

vividly clear by a few words here and there. There is an interesting chapter in the *Sentimental Journey* which perhaps partly explains how Sterne developed this gift; the passage itself is not particularly distinguished in style, but it is a good average specimen of comic narrative.

The old officer was reading attentively a small pamphlet (it might be the book of the opera) with a large pair of spectacles. As soon as I sat down, he took his spectacles off, and putting them into a shagreen case, returned them and the book into his pocket together. I half rose up, and made him a bow.

Translate this into any civilised language in the world—the sense is this: 'Here's a poor stranger come into the box—he seems as if he knew nobody; and is never likely, was he to be seven years in Paris, if every man he comes near keeps his spectacles on his nose—'tis shutting the door of conversation absolutely in his face—and using him worse than a German.'

The French officer might as well have said it all aloud; and if he had, I should in course have put the bow I made him into French too, and told him, 'I was sensible of his attention, and returned him a thousand thanks for it.'

There is not a secret so aiding to the progress of sociality, as to get master of this *short hand*, and be quick in rendering the several turns of looks and limbs, with all their inflections and delineations, into plain words. For my own part, by long habitude, I do it so mechanically, that when I walk the streets of London, I go translating all the way; and have more than once stood behind in the circle, where not three words have been said, and have brought off twenty dialogues with me, which I could have fairly wrote down and sworn to.

I was going one evening to Martini's concert at Milan, and was just entering the door of the hall, when the Marquesina de F. was coming out in a sort of a hurry—she was almost upon me before I saw her: so I gave a spring to one side to let her pass. She had done the same, and on the same side too; so we ran our heads together: she instantly got to the other side to get out: I was just as unfortunate as she had been; for I had sprung to that side, and opposed her passage again.—We both flew together to the other side, and then back—and so on—it was ridiculous; we both blushed intolerably; so I did at last the thing I should have done at first—I stood stock still, and the Marquesina had no more difficulty. I had no power to go into the room, till I had made her so much reparation as to wait and follow her with my eye to the end of the passage. She looked back twice, and walked along it rather sideways, as if she would make room for any one coming up stairs to pass her—'No,' said I, 'that's a vile translation: the Marquesina has a right to the best apology I can make her; and that opening is left for me to do it in'—so I ran and begged pardon for the embarrassment I had given her, saying it was my intention to have made her way. She answered, she was guided by the same intention towards me; so we reciprocally thanked each other. She was at the top of the stairs; and seeing no *chichisbee* near her, I begged to hand her to her coach; so we went down the stairs, stopping at every third step to talk of the concert and the adventure. 'Upon my word, madam,' said I, when I had handed her in, 'I made six different efforts to let you go out.' 'And I made six efforts,' replied she, 'to let you enter.' 'I wish to Heaven you would make a seventh,' said I. 'With all my heart,' said she, making room—Life is too short to be long about the forms of it—so I instantly stepped in, and she carried me home with her—And what became of the concert, St Cecilia, who, I suppose, was at it, knows more than I.

In the scene from *Troilus and Criseyde* there is a similar 'translation'. Criseyde lets her glance fall a little aside, as though to say, 'What, may I not stand here?' No doubt Chaucer too trained his descriptive powers by watching people's faces and movements and intepreting them to himself.

In a very austere comic style nothing more than accurate and expressive description would be needed for the narrative. This demands the ability to be direct, simple, and concise; as Chaucer is in the first few lines I quoted ('stille, allone, bihinden other folk, in litel brede, and neigh the dore'—he makes each point without fuss, patiently building up the picture). The whole stanza beginning 'She, this in blak' is a good example of the simplicity that only the most practised writers can command. But to be expressive as well as accurate a writer must find also words and phrases of power, to give life to the picture and bind it together; the words need not be uncommon, but they must awaken the imagination of the reader, and it will not be amiss if they set his heart beating a little. The word 'low' in the first line does not refer to Criseyde's stature (we learn later that she was not very small, though not at all mannish); it refers to her way of standing. 'Ay under shames drede' makes this clearer; it is not in the picture, but tells us how to put the picture together—what it means. Again, Troilus looks *thriftily* at Criseyde, and at the same time his heart *spreads and rises*; the three words bring the picture to life. Lastly, at the climax of the scene, Chaucer inserts an intensely poetical image almost in the manner of Donne: love had his dwelling *within the subtle streams of her eyes*.

Style

There is another technique equally effective but opposite in its working: I will call it analytical. The writer picks out the significant elements in a situation or a character, and leaves it to our imagination to clothe his abstractions in flesh and blood. Chaucer excelled in this style too, and in his maturity he combines it with the descriptive method. The Prologue to the *Canterbury Tales* is the classic example of this combination. In the character of the lawyer analysis predominates: all Chaucer tells us of his outside is that

> He rood but hoomly in a medlee cote
> Girt with a ceint of silk, with barres smale;

but there are two couplets of analysis which enable us to picture the man perfectly:

> Discreet he was and of greet reverence—
> He semed swich, his wordes weren so wise,

and

> No wher so bisy a man as he ther nas,
> And yet he semed bisier than he was.

He uses the same method, with a quieter touch in the famous line about the Oxford scholar,

> And gladly wolde he lerne and gladly teche.

This style, too, in its perfection, is direct, concise, and seemingly simple.

The best example of an almost purely analytical style in our comic literature is Jane Austen's narrative. Whether she could have rivalled Chaucer in description we cannot say; for she eschewed it on principle, thinking it out of place and tedious in the novel. She does describe appearances sometimes; she could hardly avoid it; but her descriptions are generally brief and bald. With a modesty in which there was some irony she declined to compete with Sir Walter Scott; what her real opinion was may be guessed from a remark of the exquisitely silly Sir Edward Denham to Charlotte Heywood in *Sanditon*,

> If Scott *has* a fault, it is the want of passion.—Tender, Elegant, Descriptive—but *Tame*.

Perhaps her art suffers from her reluctance to draw pictures. It is easy to see her characters wrongly, and for this reason Darcy (for example) is often misjudged; the illustrators draw him from Elizabeth's prejudiced impression, and not from the truth as it is revealed in the course of the story. But if Jane Austen's almost pedantic restraint leaves a door open for easy error, it makes her novels as exciting as detective stories for anyone interested in human nature.

There is a very significant paragraph in *Emma*, in chapter 27, where Emma is waiting in the doorway of Ford's the draper's, while Harriet is buying something in the shop.

> Much could not be hoped from the traffic of even the busiest part of Highbury: Mr Perry walking hastily by; Mr William Cox letting himself in at the office door; Mr Cole's carriage horses returning from exercise; or a stray letter-boy on an obstinate mule,—were the liveliest objects she could presume to expect; and when her eyes fell only on the butcher with his tray, a tidy old woman travelling homewards from shop with her full basket, two curs quarrelling over a dirty bone, and a string of dawdling children round the baker's little bow-window eyeing the gingerbread, she knew she had no reason to complain, and was amused enough; quite enough still to stand at the door. A mind lively and at ease can do with seeing nothing, and can see nothing that does not answer.

This description, of a kind very rare in her novels, is an inventory rather than a picture: and it ends with what might be taken, and was perhaps intended, as an exposition of her own philosophy, and the foundations of her art. She herself had a most lively and thorough imagination; the whole of her novels was real to her, down to the smallest detail; and there is evidence in her letters that the outsides of her characters were vividly present to her mind's eye. But she lacked, or did not develop, Chaucer's poetic gift of appealing to the senses of the reader; she 'could do with seeing nothing'. Again, at least when she was writing novels, her mind was at ease; no inhibitions distorted her understanding and judgment of human nature; everything that she could see 'answered'. What we miss is the twinkling eye of Chaucer's Friar and the shiny bald head of his Monk; the pictures of Walter Shandy with his finger on his nose, or Uncle Toby waving his pipe in the air, or Yorick leaping from his chair.

But in the analytical style Jane Austen is so great that once her

Style

art is mature the lack of pictures does not matter. Even in her early works there is not much to complain of; for example, in the passage from *Northanger Abbey* quoted on page 60. The character sketches of Mr and Mrs Bennet and Mr Collins in *Pride and Prejudice* are famous. Here is a later example, on a larger scale, from *Persuasion*; what is remarkable is that it not only tells us all about the Musgroves, but ends by telling us all about Anne herself.

> The Musgroves, like their houses, were in a state of alteration, perhaps of improvement. The father and mother were in the old English style, and the young people in the new. Mr and Mrs Musgrove were a very good sort of people; friendly and hospitable, not much educated, and not at all elegant. Their children had more modern minds and manners. There was a numerous family; but the only two grown up, excepting Charles, were Henrietta and Louisa, young ladies of nineteen and twenty, who had brought from a school at Exeter all the usual stock of accomplishments, and were now, like thousands of other young ladies, living to be fashionable, happy, and merry. Their dress had every advantage, their faces were rather pretty, their spirits extremely good, their manners unembarrassed and pleasant; they were of consequence at home, and favourites abroad. Anne always contemplated them as some of the happiest creatures of her acquaintance: but still, saved as we all are by some comfortable feeling of superiority from wishing for the possibility of exchange, she would not have given up her own more elegant and cultivated mind for all their enjoyments. . . .

A feature of this paragraph is its irony: for instance, in the first sentence, '*perhaps* of improvement'. In its quietest form, irony makes a point by what it leaves out rather than what it says; this of course leaves open to the reader a wide field of doubt and conjecture—is any irony intended, and if so what is left out that one would expect to be included? The sentence beginning 'Their dress had every advantage', suggests these questions. In the line about Criseyde on page 63:

> Honour, estat, and wommanly noblesse

(respectability, good position, and feminine good breeding), nothing is said about Criseyde's character in the deeper sense. This need not be deliberate, if the occasion does not call for more than Chaucer tells us; I think however that it does, and as the main point of the whole story is Criseyde's instability of heart (her 'slidynge corage') the omission is surely deliberate. One is always justified in looking for irony in Chaucer's comments, for it was an incorrigible habit of his; though of course that very fact may cause us to read it into some quite unironical remark. That is the danger in indulging an ironical manner of speech; it is almost certain to make one unpopular.

But Chaucer's irony is often obvious. He frequently uses the commoner method, of giving an explanation of character or conduct, which by its patent inadequacy or untruth forces us to supply the right explanation for ourselves. A good example of this kind of irony occurs in the character of the physician in the Prologue to the *Canterbury Tales*; this doctor of physic was particularly fond of gold, *because it is a valuable ingredient in medicines*. Or again, in his description of the monk:

> He yaf nat of that text a pulled hen,
> That seith that hunters ben nat hooly men,
> Ne that a monk, whan he is recchelees
> Is likned til a fish that is waterlees—
> This is to seyne, a monk out of his cloystre.
> But thilke text heeld he nat worth an oystre.
> *And I seyd his opinioun was good*——

Chaucer does not tell us what he *thought* about the attitude of this sporting churchman to the devotional and intellectual life, but only what he *said*.

Almost all comic writers use irony in some form or other. In the story quoted on pages 65–6 from the *Sentimental Journey*, the sentence 'I had no power to go into the room till I had *made her so much reparation* as to wait and follow her with my eyes' is ironical. Yorick, polite as he is, has another and stronger motive for looking after a woman who is walking away from him, and even if we did not know him well enough to smile at the phrase, the end of the story makes the irony clear. It here approaches erotic innuendo, which indeed is a form of irony, whenever its purpose is not merely to give superficial decency to an improper joke.

Of all our comic writers, Fielding is the most persistently ironical: his whole style is coloured, perhaps distorted, by irony. This suits the satirical passages, particularly the opening chapters to the different books of *Tom Jones*, and it is essential to the whole

Style

design of *Jonathan Wild*; but it gives a rather heavily facetious character to his narrative style, which becomes less attractive with each re-reading. This is a great pity, for Fielding had a comic imagination of the first order, and a very good brain. The fact is that irony more than any other literary device is subject to the law of diminishing returns. In the hands of Swift, who could keep his style at a high pitch of feeling, or Gibbon who was possessed by an inexhaustible critical curiosity, it can keep its force indefinitely; but in comedy it easily palls if it is sustained for too long, and it may end by undoing its characteristic effect. Yet tactfully used it is so nearly the exact stylistic equivalent of the comic mode of thought that I suppose nobody who enjoys and is capable of understanding comedy can fail to have a natural appreciation of it.

I have hitherto considered style only in narrative, though I pleaded on behalf of the comic novelist for his right to comment on his creations as well as to display them in action and speech. For there is a kind of comedy embodied in thought, diction, and imagery, without any story. Addison and Lamb, who are only occasionally and incidentally storytellers, are among the English comic writers; so is Max Beerbohm, not only in his stories but in his essays. In this passage from his Rede Lecture on Lytton Strachey, there is no story: the comedy is in the style alone:

We are told on high authority, from both sides of the Atlantic, that the present century is to be the Century of the Common Man. We are all of us to go down on our knees and clasp our hands and raise our eyes and worship the Common Man. I am not a learned theologian, but I think I am right in saying that this religion has at least the hall-mark of novelty —has never before been propagated, even in the East, from which so many religions have sprung. Well, I am an old man, and old men are not ready converts to new religions. This one does not stir my soul. I take some comfort in the fact that its propagators do not seek to bind us to it for ever. '*This*,' they say, 'is to be the Century of the Common Man.' I like to think that on the morning of January 1st, in the year 2000, mankind will be free to unclasp its hands and rise from its knees and look about it for some other, and perhaps more rational, form of faith.

This kind of comedy is frequently coloured by irony and it combines or unites description and analysis. To be successful it must have the same qualities of precision and clarity that Chaucer and Jane Austen have; and lacking the support of a story it can hardly dispense with imagination or fancy. It is indeed this last that marks the passage I have just quoted as comedy rather than satire; for though the criticism is of course destructive, the critic escapes from all resentment in his delight at the ludicrous image his fancy has created. This is the poetry of comedy.

In the second passage printed at the beginning of this book Coleridge claims poetic rights for comedy. The claim leads us on to Meredith's novels and his importance in the history of comedy; he attempted, alas not quite successfully, to reunite poetry to comedy, from which it had been almost completely banished since the end of the seventeenth century. Between Congreve and Meredith, Byron is the only comic poet I can think of (I do not speak of comic verse merely, but of poetic imagination, and I count Pope as a satirist rather than a comic writer); and great as Byron is, his poetry is too isolated to bridge so many years. The most notable development in our literature within the last seventy-five years has been the bringing back of poetry into the art of fiction. With the exception of Emily Brontë the great novelists of the mid-Victorian period did not more than intermittently take their readers further by their manner of writing, than the story, interestingly and sometimes energetically rendered, could take them. But in the latter half of the century two distinguished poets, Meredith and Hardy, carried their poetic gifts into prose fiction, devoting themselves to the two great traditional modes: Meredith to comedy, and Hardy to tragedy. It is curious that in doing so they both protested somewhat over much: Hardy in his ironical professions of belief in a malicious deity, Meredith by his elaborate usherings in of the Comic Spirit.

It is perhaps fairest to represent Meredith's style by samples taken from *The Egoist*, which is commonly regarded as his masterpiece. Moreover, in the Prelude to this novel he seems not only to declare his faith in comedy, but also to describe his notion of the style in which it should be written.

The chief consideration for us is, what particular practice of Art in letters is the best for the perusal of the Book of our common wisdom; so that with clearer minds and livelier manners we may escape, as it were, into daylight and song from a land of fog-horns. Shall we read it by the watchmaker's eye in luminous rings eruptive of the infinitesimal, or pointed with examples and types under the broad Alpine survey of the spirit born of our united social intelligence, which is the Comic Spirit? Wise men say the latter.

Style

In this pronouncement I understand him to be repudiating the microscopic analysis of minute detail, and advocating a style at once boldly metaphorical and subtly scientific.

The most elaborate picture I have found in *The Egoist* is this of Clara Middleton's head:

> He placed himself at a corner of the doorway for her to pass him into the house, and doated on her cheek, her ear, and the softly dusky nape of her neck, where this way and that the little lighter-coloured irreclaimable curls running truant from the comb and the knot—curls, half-curls, root-curls, vine-ringlets, wedding-rings, fledgeling feathers, tufts of down, blown wisps—waved or fell, waved over or up or involutedly, or strayed, loose and downward, in the form of small silken paws, hardly any of them much thicker than a crayon shading, cunninger than long round locks of gold to trick the heart.

It is very unlike any of Chaucer's pictures of Criseyde, also designed to give an effect of irresistible beauty. It is uncritical, very rich in feeling and associations; and it unkindly brings to mind Meredith's own phrase 'luminous rings eruptive of the infinitesimal'. The style seems inappropriate to comedy, and indeed suggests tragedy; save for the Meredithian romantic exuberance the author might be Hardy. Nor is this more impressionistic picture of Clara much nearer to comedy or further from tragedy:

> She walked back at a slow pace, and sang to herself above her darker-flowing thoughts, like the reed-warbler on the branch beside the night-stream; a simple song of a light-hearted sound, independent of the shifting black and grey of the flood underneath.

In the following short scene we seem somewhere in the border country between tragedy and comedy:

> He found himself addressing eyes that regarded him as though he were a small speck, a pin's head, in the circle of their remote contemplation. They were wide; they closed.
> She opened them to gaze elsewhere.
> He was very sensitive.
> Even then, when knowingly wounding him, or because of it, she was trying to climb back to that altitude of the thin division of neutral ground, from which we see a lover's faults and are above them, pure surveyors. She climbed unsuccessfully, it is true; soon despairing and using the effort as a pretext to fall lower.

Meredith seems as much fascinated by the penetrating power of eyes, to reach the heart, as Donne was; and he can make comedy of it, as in Crossjay's grotesque fancy, with which Clara defends her heart against the shrewd and candid but somewhat austere and awkward Vernon Whitford:

> . . . as he directed his eyes, according to his wont, penetratingly, she defended herself by fixing her mind on Robinson Crusoe's old goat in the recess of the cavern.

In another rapid simile, describing the effect of Laetitia Dale's admiration on the polished rigidity of Willoughby's character, there is excellent irony.

> The presence of Miss Dale illuminated him as the burning taper lights up consecrated plate.

But Meredith is at his best not in description, but in analysis. Here he is giving Clara's intuitions of her plight as Willoughby's fiancée; not only is she caught between the Scylla of his tenacity and the Charybdis of her father's more amiable egoism, but she finds even her own mind infected with Willoughby's shivering resentment towards mankind in general:

> Full surely this immoveable stone-man would not release her. This petrifaction of egoism would from amazedly to austerely refuse the petition. His pride would debar him from understanding her desire to be released. And if she resolved on it, without doing it straightway in Constantia's manner, the miserable bewilderment of her father, for whom such a complication would be a tragic dilemma, had to be thought of. Her father, with all his tenderness for his child, would make a stand as a point of honour; though certain to yield to her, he would be distressed, in a tempest of worry; and Dr Middleton thus afflicted threw up his arms, he shunned books, shunned speech, and resembled a castaway on the ocean, with nothing between himself and his calamity. As for the world, it would be barking at her heels. She might call the man she wrenched her hand from Egoist; jilt, the world would call her. She dwelt bitterly on her agreement with Sir Willoughby regarding the world, laying it to his charge that her garden had become a place of nettles, her horizon an unlighted fourth side of a square.

Above all it is in his own comments on his story that Meredith's style most often rises to distinction. From his own profession, these should be predominantly comic; in fact they are about equally balanced between the tragic and the comic. This seems to me tragic in tone:

> Are they not of a nature warriors, like men?—men's mates to bear them heroes instead of puppets? But the devouring male Egoist prefers them as inanimate over-wrought polished pure-metal precious vessels, fresh from the hands of the artificer, for him to walk away with hugging, call all his own, drink of, and fill and drink of, and forget that he stole them.

This begins in comedy, but ends in tragedy:

> The gift of humorous fancy is in women fenced round with forbidding placards; they have to choke it; if they perceive a piece of humour, for instance, the young Willoughby grasped by his master, and his horrified relatives rigid at the sight of preparations for the deed of sacrilege, they have to blindfold the mind's eye. They are society's hard-drilled soldiery, Prussians that must both march and think in step. It is for the advantage of the civilised world, if you like, since men have decreed it, or matrons have so read the decree; but here and there a younger woman, haply an uncorrected insurgent of the sex matured here and there, feels that her lot was cast with her head in a narrower pit than her limbs.

This is neutral, with a leaning perhaps towards comedy:

> The tempers of the young are liquid fires in isles of quicksand; the precious metals not yet cooled in a solid earth.

And the two following are admirable ironic comedy:

> Marriage has been known to have such an effect on the most faithful of women, that a great passion fades to naught in their volatile bosoms when they have taken a husband. We see in women especially the triumph of the animal over the spiritual.
>
> Weak men would be rendered nervous by the flattery of a woman's worship; or they would be for returning it, at least partially, as though it could be bandied to and fro without emulgence of the poetry; or they would be pitiful, and quite spoil the thing. Some would be for transforming the beautiful solitary vestal flame by the first effort of the multiplication-table into your hearth-fire of slippered affection. So these men are not they whom the Gods have ever selected, but rather men of a pattern with themselves, very high and very solid men, who maintain the crown by holding divinely independent of the great emotion they have sown.

I have picked these examples simply on their merits: not to demonstrate the character but only to illustrate the quality of Meredith's style. I cannot but conclude from them that it is not (like Jane Austen's or Congreve's) a style specifically attuned to comedy; but rather, like Shakespeare's, both markedly individual and also capable of expressing the widest range of moods and modes. And though in saying this I am to some extent impugning Meredith's own claim to be the especial mouthpiece of the comic spirit in his generation, it is only to make for him what is surely a higher claim.

II

In the dialogue of comedy, the aims of the writer are different: in much the same way as speech differs from the written language. Good comic dialogue is vigorous and rapid, with the manner of each speaker clearly differentiated; anything is better than flatness, and a certain crudity of caricature is not a fault. The contrast between Jane Austen's restrained and subtle narrative style and the almost vulgar high spirits of her dialogue can be most striking; it is an excellence of her art. Here is a scene from chapter 28 of *Emma*. It takes place inside Miss Bates's upstairs sitting-room.

Shortly afterwards Miss Bates, passing near the window, descried Mr Knightley on horseback, not far off.
'Mr Knightley, I declare! I must speak to him, if possible, just to thank him. I will not open the window here; it would give you all cold; but I can go into my mother's room, you know. I daresay he will come in when he knows who is here. Quite delightful to have you all meet so! Our little room so honoured!'
She was in the adjoining chamber while she still spoke, and, opening the casement there, immediately called Mr Knightley's attention, and every syllable of their conversation was as distinctly heard by the others as if it had passed within the same apartment.
'How d'ye do? How d'ye do? Very well, I thank you. So obliged to you for the carriage last night. We were just in time; my mother just ready for us. Pray come in; do come in. You will find some friends here.'
So began Miss Bates; and Mr Knightley seemed determined to be heard in his turn, for most resolutely and commandingly did he say,
'How is your niece, Miss Bates? I want to enquire after you all, but particularly your niece. How is Miss Fairfax? I hope she caught no cold last night? How is she today? Tell me how Miss Fairfax is.'

Style

And Miss Bates was obliged to give a direct answer before he would hear her in anything else. The listeners were amused; and Mrs Weston gave Emma a look of particular meaning. But Emma still shook her head in steady scepticism.

'So obliged to you!—so very much obliged to you for the carriage,' resumed Miss Bates.

He cut her short with,

'I am going to Kingston. Can I do anything for you?'

'Oh dear! Kingston—are you? Mrs Cole was saying the other day she wanted something from Kingston.'

'Mrs Cole has servants to send; can I do anything for *you*?'

'No, I thank you. But do come in. Who do you think is here? Miss Woodhouse and Miss Smith; so kind as to call to hear the new pianoforte. Do put up your horse at the Crown, and come in.'

'Well,' said he, in a deliberating manner, 'for five minutes, perhaps.'

'And here is Mrs Weston and Mr Frank Churchill too! Quite delightful! So many friends!'

'No, not now, I thank you. I could not stay two minutes. I must get on to Kingston as fast as I can.'

'Oh, do come in! They will be so very happy to see you.'

'No, no; your room is full enough. I will call another day and hear the pianoforte.'

'Well, I am so sorry! Oh Mr Knightley, what a delightful party last night! how extremely pleasant! Did you ever see such dancing? Was not it delightful? Miss Woodhouse and Mr Frank Churchill; I never saw anything equal to it.'

'Oh, very delightful indeed! I can say nothing less, for I suppose Miss Woodhouse and Mr Frank Churchill are hearing everything that passes. And' (raising his voice still more) 'I do not see why Miss Fairfax should not be mentioned too. I think Miss Fairfax dances very well; and Mrs Weston is the very best country-dance player, without exception, in England. Now, if your friends have any gratitude, they will say something pretty loud about you and me in return; but I cannot stay to hear it.'

The most noticeable thing about this scene is its stage-management; it is very dramatic, and Miss Bates and Mr Knightley are cleverly isolated from the others, so that they are both talking for effect, Miss Bates as usual unconsciously, and Mr Knightley consciously and with rather crude but telling irony. His change of manner when he hears that Frank is with the others is transparent in the extreme; such transparency is part of his character, or it would be inartistic. The novel will bear greater subtlety than this; the scene might have been written for a play. Jane Austen makes her characters talk as she wants them to; more in character than people ever talk in real life, but always in a conversational idiom. Her judgment of them is so confident that she takes the greatest pleasure in making them give themselves away. It is not, however, satire. Neither of the protagonists is unpleasant; for though Mr Knightley has been temporarily demoralised by jealousy, he gives good value to his audience. They are amused, because rude as he is to all of them, his rudeness is impartial and entertaining. This is a characteristic of good manners. The only one of the company whom one may suppose to have been embarrassed is Jane Fairfax—quite contrary to Mr Knightley's intention; it is an error of judgment in him. This increases the comedy, though it makes it a little painful.

Jane Austen can be equally dramatic in a more serious mood and quieter tone, as in the critical scene between Emma and Harriet quoted in chapter 2; the famous conversation between Lady Catherine de Burgh and Elizabeth Bennet in chapter 56 of *Pride and Prejudice* is intermediate in character between the two.

Vigour is the chief characteristic of her dialogue style; for sheer fineness of style—combining vitality with subtlety and the accurate revelation of character—her dialogue is hardly the equal of Sterne's. She excels in duologue; I cannot recall any four-fold conversation in any of her novels where the effect is both so homogeneous and also so evenly distributed between the characters as it is in the scene of Corporal Trim and the catechism. Sterne has indeed the imagination of a poet, though not the seriousness; his values are real enough, but superficial if not quite frivolous, and this shows in his essentially *prose* rhythms. Jane Austen is at the other extreme from him; *her* seriousness jibbed at poetry altogether.

But it is inevitably the dramatists who show their style most directly in dialogue; for they have nothing else to show it in. Shakespeare and Congreve are our two great dramatic stylists. Goldsmith's dialogue is clear, pure, and easy; but I have not space to do more than commend him as a rare example of artlessly excellent writing. His younger contemporary, Sheridan, can be very clever; he was a famous wit and knew all the tricks of the trade: what could be more effective than this, from *The School for Scandal?*

SIR PETER 'Slife, madam, I say, had you any of these little elegant expenses when you married me?

Style   79

LADY TEAZLE   Lud, Sir Peter, would you have me be out of the fashion?
SIR PETER   The fashion, indeed! What had you to do with the fashion before you married me?
LADY TEAZLE   For my part, I should think you would like to have your wife thought a woman of taste.
SIR PETER   Ay—there again—taste.—Zounds! madam, you had no taste when you married me.
LADY TEAZLE   That's very true indeed, Sir Peter; and after having married you, I should never pretend to taste again. . . .

It is brilliant, but a little obvious. Nevertheless, good craftsmanship deserves its reward, especially in the theatre, which of all things should shun dullness; it is one thing to see through Sheridan, and another to be able to do what he can do. But with Shakespeare and Congreve we are on another level.

III

Shakespeare is a writer so great and original that no moral can be drawn from his practice except the moral Coleridge drew from the practice of all poets: that there is no rule of style, and that the only laws by which a poet should be guided are those of the imagination. Shakespeare developed his dramatic style by constant experiment and assimilation, and used whatever kind of poetry or prose served his immediate purpose, regardless of whether he was writing a comedy or a tragedy. In two plays written about the same time—*Romeo and Juliet* and *A Midsummer Night's Dream*—there is a mixture of precisely the same elements: imaginative nature poetry, a burlesque 'tragic' style, and a brusque humorous prose; yet the one is a tragedy and the other a comedy. In apparent disregard of propriety his tragedies abound in intellectual wit and homely common sense, and his comedies in sensuous poetry and emotional rhetoric. These four categories—sensuous poetry, wit, rhetoric, and common sense—are not very scientifically exact and not mutually exclusive; but they provide a convenient scheme for so rapid a glance as this must be at the style of Shakespeare's comedies.

In the scene from *A Midsummer Night's Dream* quoted in chapter 2, and more strikingly in other scenes from the same play, Shakespeare puts into Titania's mouth that poetry of the senses which was the foundation of his dramatic language; it is not particularly well adapted to comic uses, except when the situation gives it, as in this scene, a character of burlesque. It is used in a similar way in *As You Like It*, for Silvius and Phebe, where it is rather wasted on two characters who only exist in order to be scolded by Rosalind. In *Twelfth Night* Shakespeare is very lavish with it, and very skilful in making dramatic use of it—for the sentimental Orsino, the romantic Viola, and (by a species of dramatic irony) for coldhearted Olivia when she has been wakened into life by falling in love with 'Cesario'. But even in so urban a play as *Much Ado About Nothing* it appears by flashes:

> Good morrow, masters; put your torches out:
> The *wolves have prey'd;* and look, the gentle day,
> Before the wheels of Phœbus, round about
> *Dapples the drowsy east with spots of grey.*

or

> Good morrow, Benedick. Why, what's the matter
> That you have such a *February* face,
> *So full of frost, of storm, and cloudiness?*

In fact, Shakespeare uses it in all his plays from first to last, and it must be accepted as an ingredient in his comic style.

This kind of poetry has a profound effect on any play in which it appears even for a moment: and the most superficial attention to the style of Shakespeare's comedies raises again the question discussed in my last chapter—whether these comedies not only differ in quality from all other comedies (that is obvious), but belong to a totally different kind. Ben Jonson implies a criticism of Shakespeare's comic style when he uses the expressions 'deeds and *language such as men do use*', and '*an image of the times*', in the prologue to *Everyman in his Humour*. To the shade of Jonson, and to anyone who shares his misgivings but stifles them because of Shakespeare's reputation, I would reply by a misapplication of the lines spoken by Caliban in *The Tempest*:

> Be not afear'd; the isle is full of noises,
> Sounds and sweet airs, that give delight and hurt not.

The 'wheels of Phœbus' do not help much towards the comedy; but one need not be afraid of them—they give delight and hurt not.

Style 81

We may rightly picture comedy as played within the four walls of human habitation; but if the dramatist chooses to remind us by his imagery that there is something outside—say, the wolves, or the frost and storm—he will not thereby necessarily weaken the effect and value of the comedy. I have accounted partly for the range of Shakespeare's comic world by the place the *average* Elizabethan instinctively assigned to man in the universe. But not all the Elizabethans were so consistently poetical as Shakespeare; and I have said that even Chaucer, who lived in a period certainly no more given to narrow materialism than Shakespeare's, is not so cosmic in his range as Shakespeare. Ultimately this is a question of taste, not to be decided on theoretical grounds. One can be grateful for the richness of Shakespeare's style, but at the same time feel free to criticise the detail of particular plays.

So far as Shakespeare uses the poetry of the senses to give life and definition to his scene, he is putting it to a use strictly appropriate to comedy; as Chaucer had done before him and Congreve did after him. Chaucer of course uses it mainly in his narrative; the two later writers are forced to use it in dialogue if at all. In that respect Chaucer had an easier task; it is no doubt more difficult to be both poetical and colloquial than to be poetical and descriptive. But when Don Pedro speaks of Benedick's '*February* face' we scarcely notice the difficulty; so great is Shakespeare's mastery.

The second main ingredient in Shakespeare's style, his intellectual wit, is more particularly appropriate to comedy. Here we have his equivalent to the analytical styles of Chaucer and Jane Austen; but his is more sententious and elaborate, in fact, Elizabethan. It is seen at its best in Benedick's soliloquy in *Much Ado*, when he has been tricked into believing that Beatrice is in love with him.

They seem to pity the lady: it seems her affections have their full bent. Love me! why, it must be requited. I hear how I am censured: they say I will bear myself proudly, if I perceive the love come from her; they say too that she will rather die than give any sign of affection. I did never think to marry. I must not seem proud: happy are they that hear their detractions, and can put them to mending. They say the lady is fair,—'tis a truth, I can bear them witness. And virtuous,—'tis so, I cannot reprove it. And wise, but for loving me,—by my troth, it is no addition to her wit, nor no great argument of her folly, for I will be horribly in love with her. I may chance have some odd quirks and remnants of wit broken on me, because I have railed so long against marriage: but doth not the appetite alter? a man loves the meat in his youth that he cannot endure in his age. Shall quips and sentences and these paper bullets of the brain awe a man from the career of his humour? No, the world must be peopled. When I said I would die a bachelor, I did not think I should live till I were married. . . .

In chapter 2 I referred to this speech as an example of 'internal' comedy: comedy embodied in the thoughts of a single character. By the free use of soliloquy Shakespeare was able to display such internal drama, both in his tragedies and comedies; but its ancestry in comedy may be seen by a quotation from John Lyly's famous novel, *Euphues*. Lucilla is making up her mind to throw Philautus over in favour of Euphues, and her thoughts are put into the form of a soliloquy:

But suppose that Euphues love thee, that Philautus leave thee, will thy father, thinkest thou, give thee liberty to live after thine own lust? Will he esteem him worthy to inherit his possessions whom he accounteth unworthy to enjoy thy person? Is it like that he will match thee in marriage with a stranger, with a Grecian, with a mean man? Ay, but what knoweth my father whether he be wealthy, whether his revenues be able to countervail my father's lands, whether his birth be noble, yea or no? Can anyone make doubt of his gentle blood that seeth his gentle conditions? Can his honour be called into question whose honesty is so great? Is he to be thought thriftless who in all qualities of the mind is peerless? No, no; the tree is known by his fruit, the gold by his touch, the son by the sire. And as the soft wax receiveth whatsoever print be in the seal and showeth no other impression, so the tender babe being sealed with his father's gifts representeth his image most lively. But were I once certain of Euphues' good will, I would not so superstitiously account of my father's ill will. Time hath weaned me from my mother's teat and age rid me from my father's correction; when children are in their swathe clothes then are they subject to the whip and ought to be careful of the rigour of their parents. As for me, seeing I am not fed with their pap, I am not to be led by their persuasions. Let my father use what speeches he list, I will follow mine own lust—lust, Lucilla, what sayest thou? no, no, mine own love I should have said, for I am as far from lust as I am from reason, and as near to love as I am to folly. Then stick to thy determination, and show thyself what love can do, what love dares do, what love hath done. Albeit I can no way quench the coals of desire with forgetfulness, yet will I rake them up in the ashes of modesty; seeing I dare not discover my love for maidenly shamefastness, I will dissemble it till time I have opportunity. And I hope so to behave myself as Euphues shall think me his own, and

Style

Philautus persuade himself I am none but his. But I would to God Euphues would repair hither, that the sight of him might mitigate some part of my martyrdom.

We cannot perhaps share the inexhaustible delight of the Elizabethans in word-patterns; but Euphuism was certainly of the utmost value in originating a modern English comic style: its effect can be felt more than a century later, in Congreve. And Lyly's influence on Shakespeare was great and salutary. The other two main influences on his comic drama—Latin comedy and the Italian novel —might without Lyly have led to the *Comedy of Errors*, and even *Measure for Measure*: but it was from Lyly's comedies that he advanced both to *Much Ado* and to *As You Like It*. And the superiority of Benedick's soliloquy to Lucilla's came only with time and practice. Here is an early and inferior example: the soliloquy of Biron (the hero of *Love's Labour's Lost*, and the most interesting of Shakespeare's early comic characters), when he, like Benedick, has gone the way of the world.

The King he is hunting the deer; I am coursing myself: they have pitched a toil; I am toiling in a pitch—pitch that defiles: defile! a foul word. Well, sit thee down, sorrow! for so they say the fool said, and so say I, and I the fool: well proved, wit! By the Lord, this love is as mad as Ajax: it kills sheep, it kills me, I a sheep: well proved again, o' my side! I will not love: if I do, hang me; i' faith I will not. Oh but her eye,—by this light, but for her eye, I would not love her; yes, for her two eyes. Well, I do nothing in the world but lie, and lie in my throat. By heaven, I do love: and it hath taught me to rhyme, and to be melancholy; and here is part of my rhyme, and here my melancholy. Well, she hath one o' my sonnets already: the clown bore it, the fool sent it, and the lady hath it: sweet clown, sweeter fool, sweetest lady! By the world, I would not care a pin, if the other three were in. Here comes one with a paper: God give him grace to groan!

The wit of this passage is inferior to Lyly's: there is nothing in it half so good as 'raking the coals of desire up in the ashes of modesty'. It is more like Nashe, and like Nashe's style it has a colloquial energy and crudity which make it more dramatic than Lyly's. All these writers were infected with the Elizabethan passion for playing with words. It is well (in the long run) that they were; but it makes them all at times both tiresome and tedious. We could spare much of the back-chat between Shakespeare's characters, even Benedick and Beatrice, and be none the worse.

The third main element in Shakespeare's dramatic style was also, like the other two I have mentioned, characteristically Elizabethan. It is a long-winded (in the good as well as in the bad sense) rhetoric in verse, much used by Shakespeare in his early comedies and in his history plays; its effect is to hold up the action and reinforce the dramatic effect by a generalising poetry linking the limited subject of the play to a more comprehensive view. The best-known of these speeches are Jaques's 'All the world's a stage', and Portia's 'The quality of mercy is not strained'. The development and steady increase in power of this Shakespearean verse-rhetoric plays a most important part in the maturing of his style, especially in comedy. It may be roughly gauged by comparing Biron's 76-line speech in *Love's Labour's Lost*, Act IV, scene iii, with Portia's famous speech, and both of them with Prospero's 'Our revels now are ended' in *The Tempest*. I quote a part of Biron's speech.

> Other slow arts entirely keep the brain,
> And therefore, finding barren practisers,
> Scarce show a harvest of their heavy toil;
> But love, first learned in a lady's eyes,
> Lives not alone immured in the brain,
> But with the motion of all elements,
> Courses as swift as thought in every power,
> And gives to every power a double power,
> Above their functions and their offices.
> It adds a precious seeing to the eye:
> A lover's eyes will gaze an eagle blind;
> A lover's ear will hear the lowest sound,
> When the suspicious head of theft is stopp'd;
> Love's feeling is more soft and sensible
> Than are the tender horns of cockled snails;
> Love's tongue proves dainty Bacchus gross in taste.
> For valour, is not Love a Hercules
> Still climbing trees in the Hesperides?
> Subtle as Sphinx? as sweet and musical
> As bright Apollo's lute strung with his hair?
> And when Love speaks, the voice of all the gods
> Makes heaven drowsy with the harmony.
> Never durst poet touch a pen to write
> Until his ink were tempered with Love's sighs;

Style

> Oh, then his lines would ravish savage ears,
> And plant in tyrants mild humility:
> From women's eyes this doctrine I derive;
> They sparkle still the right Promethean fire;
> They are the books, the arts, the academes,
> That show, contain, and nourish all the world,
> Else none at all in aught proves excellent.

Here the weight of sense and experience is hardly sufficient to carry the energy of thought and feeling; the poet sets one human organ after another in motion and presses all the gods into his platonic orchestra, although the speaker himself (this is the theme of the play) is only half in earnest. Portia's eloquence, on the other hand, is not only attuned to matter of graver concern, it is also more restrained and muscular. And Prospero's, with deeper experience behind it than either of the other two, combines the imaginative richness of the first with an even greater economy of effort and material than that of the second.

The crucial step in this development came not in Shakespeare's comedies, but in his later history plays. In these plays, especially in *Henry IV* and *Henry V*, he faced the political implications of human nature; and this forced into his style, almost against his will, an ungraceful but most efficient hardness. This is seen most clearly, I think, in that disagreeable play, *Henry V*, in such a speech as 'Once more unto the breach', which is so hackneyed that its stylistic significance has been neglected.

> In peace there's nothing so becomes a man
> As modest stillness and humility:
> But when the blast of war blows in our ears,
> Then imitate the action of the tiger;
> Stiffen the sinews, summon up the blood,
> Disguise fair nature with hard-favoured rage. . . .

This hardness marks a period in Shakespeare's mental development and gives him a new strength, from which his fully mature comedies benefited. I add to the examples I have already given a well-known speech from *Measure for Measure*, when Shakespeare's style had matured.

> Be absolute for death; either death or life
> Shall thereby be the sweeter. Reason thus with life:
> If I do lose thee, I do lose a thing

> That none but fools would keep. A breath thou art
> Servile to all the skyey influences,
> That dost this habitation where thou keep'st
> Hourly afflict. Merely, thou art death's fool;
> For him thou labour'st by thy flight to shun,
> And yet runn'st towards him still. Thou art not noble;
> For all the accommodations that thou bear'st
> Are nursed by baseness. Thou'rt by no means valiant;
> For thou dost fear the soft and tender fork
> Of a poor worm. Thy best of rest is sleep,
> And that thou oft provokest; yet grossly fear'st
> Thy death, which is no more. Thou art not thyself;
> For thou exist'st on many a thousand grains
> That issue out of dust. Happy thou art not;
> For what thou has not still thou striv'st to get,
> And what thou hast forget'st. Thou art not certain;
> For thy complexion shifts to strange effects
> After the moon. If thou art rich, thou'rt poor;
> For, like an ass whose back with ingots bows,
> Thou bear'st thy heavy riches but a journey,
> And death unloads thee. Friend hast thou none;
> For thine own bowels, which do call thee sire,
> The mere effusion of thy proper loins,
> Do curse the gout, serpigo, and the rheum,
> For ending thee no sooner. Thou hast nor youth nor age,
> But, as it were an after-dinner's sleep,
> Dreaming on both; for all thy blessed youth
> Becomes as aged, and doth beg the alms
> Of palsied eld; and when thou art old and rich,
> Thou has neither heat, affection, limb nor beauty,
> To make thy riches pleasant. What's yet in this,
> That bears the name of life? Yet in this life
> Lie hid moe thousand deaths: yet death we fear,
> That makes these odds all even.

Rhetoric is a valuable element in comedy; and of course it need not be in verse. Shaw uses it regularly, to excellent effect; he has been criticised for doing so, with less reason than pedantry and ignorance. Indeed, without these larger units of thought and feeling it is perhaps impossible for comedy to rise to its full height. I need scarcely add that they are strictly dramatic; they do not represent the author's considered philosophy, but arise out of the temperament of the speaker, or the situation.

Style

As for the element of homely and prosaic common sense in Shakespeare's style, it was native to him. He always loved natural sentiments expressed in plain downright English. Such good sense he introduced into his earlier comedies under the disguise of simplicity, in characters like Bottom ('Not so neither; but if I had wit enough to get out of this wood, I have enough to serve my turn'). But just as the discipline of the history plays matured his rhetoric, so it seems also to have strengthened the fibre of his shorter speeches. In *As You Like It* and *Twelfth Night* a new vigour comes into his comic dialogue, without distinction of persons. All the ornament seems to drop away, unless there is a true dramatic reason for it, as in some of Touchstone's speeches. This is the highest kind of comic wit: an exact and satisfying correspondence of manner to matter, combined with extreme economy of words. Rosalind has a directness of speech hardly to be found in any of Shakespeare's plays before *As You Like It*:

> If that I do not dream, or be not frantic,—
> As I do trust I am not,—then dear uncle,
> Never so much as in a thought unborn
> Did I offend your Highness.

This plain style is most effective in prose. It produces some of the most famous pregnant sayings in Shakespeare: Touchstone's reply to the bravado of Rosalind ('Well, this is the forest of Arden'):

> Ay, now am I in Arden; the more fool I; when I was at home I was in a better place——

Jaques's:

> I do not desire you to please me; I do desire you to sing——

Rosalind's rejoinder to Jaques:

And your experience makes you sad! I had rather have a fool to make me merry than experience to make me sad.—And to travel for it, too!——

Sir Toby's hit at Malvolio in *Twelfth Night*:

Dost thou think, because thou art virtuous, there shall be no more cakes and ale?——

Pompey's brave words to Mistress Overdone in *Measure for Measure*, when she has fallen on evil days:

Courage! there will be pity taken on you: you that have worn your eyes almost out in the service, you will be considered.

and so right up to the end of Shakespeare's career, with Autolycus in *The Winter's Tale*:

> If I had a mind to be honest, I see Fortune would not suffer me: She drops booties in my mouth.

But it is to be found in Shakespeare's latest verse, too, in easy juxtaposition with all the other elements of his style:

> This island's mine, by Sycorax my mother,
> Which thou tak'st from me. When thou camest first
> Thou strok'dst me and mad'st much of me; would'st give me
> Water with berries in't, and teach me how
> To name the bigger light, and how the less,
> That burn by day and night. And then I loved thee,
> And showed thee all the qualities o' the isle,
> The fresh springs, brine-pits, barren place and fertile:
> Curse'd be I that I did so!

Easy as it looks, this dramatic and pregnant plainness marks the highest level of Shakespeare's comic style.

IV

Shakespeare's style developed continuously; it is impossible to talk of his comic style as of something distinct from his tragic style; one can pick out this or that element as more appropriate to comedy or to tragedy, but none that is confined to either. But Congreve's is an essentially comic style; it seemed obvious at the beginning of this chapter to go to him for characteristic examples of comic imagery and rhythm.

He had the advantage that the society for and about which he wrote was a society of wits; his ear was tuned to lively and intelligent conversation. Not only was the lowest standard of educated talk higher than among us, but for that very reason it was more necessary to discriminate between true and false wit. Perhaps also he benefited from belonging to a less insecure period than the Restoration dramatists; he was a contemporary of Swift, Pope, and Addison, and I think it is possible to discern in his plays a wider horizon than in Wycherley's or Etherege's or even Dryden's. But any advantages he may have derived from good fortune cannot account for his unrivalled superiority over every other dramatist of his lifetime. It is a superiority of style; of a wit personal to Congreve and different in kind from that of his nearest rival, Etherege; of a highly critical intelligence and acutely sensitive perceptions.

Meredith says that *The Way of the World* 'has no idea in it, beyond the stale one, that so the world goes'; as though he had been unable to see further into the play than its title, which he did not understand. It is an old proverb, at least as old as the *Roman de la Rose*:

> All the world holdith this wey;
> Love makith all to goon miswey;

and since Meredith himself is fond of this theme, he could hardly have called it stale if he had known the meaning of the proverb. It is true, however, that Congreve's plays embody a mentality rather than a philosophy: that their consistency is emotional and aesthetic, not systematic and theoretical like Ben Jonson's.

Congreve was both fastidious and good-natured: a rare combination, and of the best possible omen for comedy. The same blend is to be found in Chaucer and Jane Austen; they are all three good-natured, with the real good nature that can hate what is hateful, fiercely and whole-heartedly. Congreve hates malice: the deeply-rooted selfish malice of Fainall, as well as the shallow malice of Witwoud. This comes out in the style of his dialogue: in this scene (Act I, scene iii of *The Way of the World*), for instance.

FAINALL Joy of your Success, Mirabell; you look pleas'd.
MIRABELL Ay; I have been engag'd in a Matter of some sort of Mirth, which is not yet ripe for Discovery. I am glad this is not a Cabal-Night. I wonder, Fainall, that you who are married, and of consequence should be discreet, will suffer your Wife to be of such a Party.
FAINALL Faith, I am not jealous. Besides, most who are engag'd are

Women and Relations; and for the Men, they are of a Kind too contemptible to give Scandal.
MIRABELL   I am of another Opinion. The greater the Coxcomb, always the more the Scandal; for a Woman who is not a Fool, can have but one Reason for associating with a Man who is one.
FAINALL   Are you jealous as often as you see Witwoud entertain'd by Millamant?
MIRABELL   Of her Understanding I am, if not of her Person.
FAINALL   You do her wrong; for to give her her Due, she has Wit.
MIRABELL   She has Beauty enough to make any Man think so; and Complaisance enough not to contradict him who shall tell her so.
FAINALL   For a passionate Lover, methinks you are a Man somewhat too discerning in the Failings of your Mistress.
MIRABELL   And for a discerning Man, somewhat too passionate a Lover; for I like her with all her Faults; nay, like her for her Faults. Her Follies are so natural, or so artful, that they become her; and those Affectations which in another Woman wou'd be odious serve but to make her more agreeable. I'll tell thee, Fainall, she once us'd me with that Insolence, that in Revenge I took her to pieces; sifted her, and separated her Failings; I study'd 'em and got 'em by Rote. The Catalogue was so large, that I was not with Hopes, one Day or other to hate her heartily: to which end I so us'd myself to think of 'em, that at length, contrary to my Design and Expectation, they gave me ev'ry Hour less and less Disturbance; 'till in a few Days it became habitual to me, to remember 'em without being displeas'd. They are now grown as familiar to me as my own Frailties; and in all probability in a little time longer I shall like 'em as well.
FAINALL   Marry her, marry her; be half as well acquainted with her Charms, as you are with her Defects, and my Life on't, you are your own Man again.
MIRABELL   Say you so?
FAINALL   Ay, ay, I have Experience: I have a Wife, and so forth.

I have chosen to illustrate Congreve's good nature first, because it was the quality that most impressed his contemporaries, and has least justice done to it today. It is the more important because good nature is really essential to the comic mode; without it comedy sinks to the level of satire, and with it a satirist can rise to the level of comedy. But the most characteristic quality of Congreve's style is not so much good nature as gaiety and high spirits. He was a very young man when he wrote his plays, and it is quite proper that they should be irreverent, especially towards the elderly, as in this scene from *Love for Love*, where Angelica is ragging her uncle and her cousin's nurse. Foresight is described in the Dramatis Personae as 'an illiterate old fellow, peevish and positive, superstitious and pretending to understand astrology, palmistry, physiognomy, omens, dreams, etc.'.

ANGELICA Will you lend me your Coach? or I'll go on—Nay, I'll declare how you prophesied Popery was coming, only because the Butler had mislaid some of the Apostle Spoons, and thought they were lost. Away went Religion and Spoonmeat together. Indeed, Uncle, I'll indict you for a Wizard.
FORESIGHT How, Hussy! was there ever such a provoking Minx?
NURSE O merciful Father, how she talks!
ANGELICA Yes, I can make Oath of your unlawful Midnight Practices: you and the old Nurse there——
NURSE Marry Heav'n defend—I at Midnight Practices—O Lord, what's here to do?—I in unlawful Doings with my Master's Worship—Why, did you ever hear the like now—Sir, did ever I do anything of your Midnight Concerns—but warm your Bed, and tuck you up, and set the Candle and your Tobacco-box and your Urinal by you, and now and then rub the Soles of your Feet? O Lord, I!——
ANGELICA Yes, I saw you together thro' the Key-hole of the Closet, one Night, like Saul and the Witch of Endor, turning the Sieve and Shears, and pricking your Thumbs, to write poor innocent Servants' Names in Blood, about a little Nutmeg-grater which she had forgot in the caudle cup—Nay, I know something worse, if I would speak of it.
FORESIGHT I defy you, Hussy; but I'll remember this, I'll be revenged on you, Cockatrice; I'll hamper you—you have your Fortune in your own Hands—but I'll find a way to make your Lover, your Prodigal Spendthrift Gallant, Valentine, pay for all, I will.
ANGELICA Will you? I care not, but all shall out then—Look to't, Nurse; I can bring witness that you have a great unnatural Teat under your left Arm, and he another; and that you suckle a young Devil in the Shape of a Tabby-cat, by turns, I can.
NURSE A Teat, a Teat, I an unnatural Teat! O the false slanderous thing; feel, feel here, if I have anything but like another Christian [*crying*].

This is not ill-natured; but it is merciless. Congreve was only beginning in this play to discriminate between slowness of wit, silliness, and knavery: even if he had never learnt it he would have been a delightful, but scarcely perhaps a great, comic writer. His triumphs of discrimination are Lady Wishfort and Sir Wilful

Witwoud in *The Way of the World*—both of whom receive the most exact comic justice.

There is gaiety of another kind in the conversations between Mirabell and Millamant: a delight in the clash between two friends of very different temperament and of opposite sexes: in that sort of equal and drawn battle that makes for the highest comedy. As here:

MILLAMANT   Mirabell, did you take Exceptions last Night? O ay, and went away—Now I think on't I'm angry—No, now I think on't I'm pleased—For I believe I gave you some Pain.
MIRABELL   Does that please you?
MILLAMANT   Infinitely; I love to give Pain.
MIRABELL   You wou'd affect a Cruelty which is not in your Nature; your true Vanity is in the Power of pleasing.
MILLAMANT   O I ask your Pardon for that—One's Cruelty is one's Power, and when one parts with one's Cruelty, one parts with one's Power; and when one has parted with that, I fancy one's old and ugly.
MIRABELL   Ay, ay, suffer your Cruelty to ruin the Object of your Power, to destroy your Lover—And then how vain, how lost a Thing you'll be! Nay, 'tis true: you are no longer handsome when you've lost your Lover; your Beauty dies upon the Instant: for Beauty is the Lover's Gift; 'tis he bestows your Charms—your Glass is all a Cheat. The Ugly and the Old, whom the Looking-glass mortifies, yet after Commendation can be flatter'd by it, and discover Beauties in it: for that reflects our Praises, rather than your Face.
MILLAMANT   O the Vanity of these Men! Fainall, d'ye hear him? If they did not commend us, we were not handsome! Now you must know they cou'd not commend one, if one was not handsome. Beauty the Lover's Gift—Lord, what is a Lover, that it can give? Why one makes Lovers as fast as one pleases, and they live as long as one pleases, and they die as soon as one pleases: and then if one pleases one makes more.
WITWOUD   Very pretty. Why, you make no more of making of Lovers, Madam, than of making so many Card-matches.
MILLAMANT   One no more owes one's Beauty to a Lover than one's Wit to an Echo: they can but reflect what we look and say; vain empty Things if we are silent or unseen, and want a Being.
MIRABELL   Yet, to those two vain empty Things, you owe two of the greatest Pleasures of your Life.
MILLAMANT   How so?
MIRABELL   To your Lover, you owe the Pleasure of hearing yourselves prais'd, and to an Echo the Pleasure of hearing yourselves talk.

The superficial character of Congreve's style is well described by

Style

Meredith: 'He hits the mean of a fine style and a natural dialogue. He is at once precise and voluble.' Professor Dobrée has rightly stressed and well illustrated its poetic beauty. Congreve's language is not merely brilliant, but brilliantly *expressive* and beautifully musical. My own favourite example is the very short one quoted on page 60: the image as well as the two adjectives ('violent' and 'inflexible') are beyond the range of any but the highest poetic imagination: unexcelled by Chaucer or Shakespeare.

I must stress one particular quality of Congreve, in the face of a common misunderstanding. His dialogue, some say, is extremely polished, graceful, and beautiful to listen to; but it lacks the crude vigour necessary for the theatre; a comedy by Congreve is a string of conversations rather than a play. We have heard less of the criticism since Sir Nigel Playfair refuted it by his revivals of *The Way of the World* and *The Old Bachelor*. Experience has proved that Congreve's style cries out, not only to be spoken, but to be put into the mouths of actors.

He was a very bold and original dramatist, with little respect for the proprieties of dramatic technique to which so much importance was attached in the late seventeenth century. He used soliloquies and asides frequently; and though his setting was always (unlike Shakespeare's) a real-life setting, and his characters were drawn from the society of his times, he allowed himself to handle them in a spirit of fantasy, as when Sir Wilful Witwoud takes off his boots in the drawing-room, or in the scene I have quoted from *Love for Love*. He has nothing of the crude and tense violence of his older contemporary Wycherley, whose sense of theatre was in many ways superior to Congreve's. What is dramatic in Congreve is the texture of his plays. The accent of each speaker is distinguished by subtle gradations of rhythm and idiom. In *The Old Bachelor* this is not so well done as in his later plays when he had more experience; that is natural. He does not in this play create original characters or scenes, but relies on the old stock types and stock situations. And he is too much in love with his own style: a healthy symptom in a young writer, but nevertheless a fault. The metaphors and similes which throughout his career he used as his chief means of expression (and very fine they are) are too frequent and relished too much for their own sake. He had not learnt the restraint a dramatist has to learn, to put the right words into the mouths of the different characters. Wit came so easy to him that he could not resist the temptation to make even his fools witty, as in this reply of Sir Joseph Wittol to Sharper:

SHARPER ... Money is but Dirt, Sir Joseph—mere Dirt.
SIR JOSEPH But I profess 'tis a Dirt I have washed my Hands of at present——

a perfect answer, but much too good for Sir Joseph. But even in this play the characters stand out in sharp relief, however commonplace they may be in conception.

Above all he excelled (like Shakespeare) in the use of set speeches which crystallise the characters in miniature. This was a device, or talent, that Congreve used from the first; it is almost as fully developed in *The Old Bachelor* as in *The Way of the World*. One such speech is Lady Pliant's in *The Double-Dealer*, quoted on page 60; another is Mirabell's 'And for a discerning man, somewhat too passionate a lover. . . .' (see page 90). Here is one from Sir Joseph Wittol, speaking this time for himself and not for Congreve.

Gads-Daggers-Belts-Blades and Scabbards, this is the very Gentleman! How shall I make him a Return suitable to the Greatness of his Merit—I had a pretty thing to that purpose, if he hadn't frightened it out of my Memory.—Hem! hem! Sir, I most submissively implore your Pardon for my Transgression of Ingratitude and Omission; having my entire Dependence, Sir, upon the superfluity of your Goodness, which, like an Inundation, will, I hope, totally immerge the recollection of my Error, leaving me floating in your Sight upon the full blown Bladders of Repentance—by the help of which I shall once more hope to swim into your Favour.

Here is Sir Sampson Legend, the incompetent bullying father in *Love for Love*:

VALENTINE I would have an Excuse for your Barbarity and unnatural Usage.
SIR SAMPSON Excuse! Impudence! Why, sirrah, mayn't I do what I please? Are not you my Slave? Did I not beget you? And might not I have chosen whether I would have begot you or not? 'Oons, who are you? Whence came you? What brought you into the World? How came you here sir? Here, to stand here, upon those two Legs, and look erect with that audacious Face, hah? Answer me that. Did you come a Volunteer into the World? Or did I, with the lawful Authority of a Parent, press you to the Service?

Style

Almost any of Lady Wishfort's speeches would serve to expose the nakedness of her pathetic naïveté; her outbursts of 'boudoir Billingsgate' are famous; but perhaps this is the best example:

> Well, and how shall I receive him? In what Figure shall I give his Heart the first Impression? There is a great deal in the first Impression. Shall I sit?—No, I won't sit—I'll walk—ay, I'll walk from the Door upon his Entrance; and then turn full upon him—No, that will be too sudden: I'll lie—ay, I'll lie down—I'll receive him in my little Dressing-room, there's a Couch—Yes, yes, I'll give the first Impression on a Couch—I won't lie, neither, but loll and lean upon one Elbow; with one Foot a little dangling off, jogging in a thoughtful way—yes—and then as soon as he appears, start, ay, start and be surpris'd, and rise to meet him in a pretty Disorder—Yes—O, nothing is more alluring than a Levee from a Couch in some Confusion—It shews the Foot to advantage, and furnishes with Blushes and recomposing Airs beyond Comparison. . . .

And one last example from *The Way of the World*:

> WITWOUD Come, come, you are malicious now, and wou'd breed Debates.—Petulant's my Friend, and a very honest Fellow, and a very pretty Fellow, and has a smattering—Faith and Troth a pretty deal of an odd sort of a small Wit: nay, I'll do him Justice. I'm his Friend, I won't wrong him.—And if he had any Judgment in the World—he wou'd not be altogether contemptible. Come, come don't detract from the Merits of my Friend.

5

CHARACTER AND PLOT

I

Opinions about the value of comedy are much influenced by the technique of particular writers. Because a comedy by Shakespeare almost always ends with a marriage, it is generally supposed that the purpose of comedy is to encourage optimism, or at least cheerfulness. The tradition of ending with a marriage was not invented by Shakespeare; but the popular view of comedy in England is no doubt based on a sentimental response to *As You Like It, All's Well that Ends Well, The Tempest*, and other Shakespearean plays. This is only one example of our tendency to judge works of fiction more mechanically than, for example, lyrical poems. A lyric is short, and apparently more direct in saying what it has to say; we usually have some idea what it is about, even after a single reading. A play or a novel is much longer, and less explicit; and readers with a little knowledge of the technique of fiction easily form the habit of judging it by certain simple analytical tests. This habit is encouraged by critics, who use the same tests, sometimes fairly scientifically, but sometimes also rather arbitrarily. Analytical tests are valuable, perhaps necessary; but only if we understand their origin, and the principles for applying them.

Our concepts of plot and character as separate entities in fiction derive from Aristotle's *Poetics:* but the *Poetics* is a treatise on tragedy, and it is not safe to assume that Aristotle would have made the same generalisations about comedy. He was a teleological philosopher; in discussing anything, he always had in mind the ultimate question 'What is it for?'. But at the same time he was fond of analysis, and had a somewhat dangerous propensity to

Character and plot 97

dissect things into their parts: dangerous, that is to say, to any reader who has not the thorough grasp of the subject that Aristotle had. He himself insisted, as much as any critic ever has done, on the need for unity in a work of art. And lastly, he was generalising about *Greek* tragedy, with which many modern readers are unfamiliar, and which differed drastically from modern fiction both in subject matter and in function. In these circumstances, therefore, the *Poetics* is a most valuable point of departure for the modern critic; but no more.

The passage which originated the analytical examination of works of fiction occurs in chapter 6 of the *Poetics*. I translate it as follows:

As the story is composed to be acted, it would follow of necessity that one element in a tragedy must be the Mise en scène. Others are Music and Language, for these are the media in which the play is composed. By Language I mean merely the words of the play; and every one knows what is meant by Music. Again, since the subject matter of the play is a story, and there must be persons to take part in it, whose personality will be determined by their Character and Intelligence—for these are the factors we have in mind when we define the quality of their actions—it follows that there are two natural causes of the story, Intelligence and Character, and that the success or failure of all the persons in it must accord with these two factors. Now the Fable is the presentation of the story; and by Fable I mean the synthesis of the action. By Character I mean the factor that defines what sort of people the participants in the story are; and Intelligence is shown in their whole manner of expressing themselves when they are making a statement or disclosing an opinion. There are therefore necessarily six elements in every tragedy, which give it its quality: and they are the Fable, Character, Intelligence, the Mise en scène, Language and Music. The first three are the subject matter of the art, the fourth the manner of its presentation, and the last two the medium in which it is composed; and there is no other element in tragedy besides these.

Aristotle goes on to argue that the 'synthesis of the action' is the most important element in the art of tragic drama. 'What happens, that is the Fable, is the end of tragedy; and the end of anything is the most important consideration.' His answer to the question, 'What is tragedy for?' is 'The Fable'. Of the other elements in tragic art he considers characterisation the most important.

The word I have translated by 'Fable' is *mythos:* a word of which the English 'plot' always seems to me an inadequate

D

rendering. It is true that Aristotle defines the *mythos* of a tragedy as 'the synthesis of the action', which is a pretty exact definition of what we commonly understand by the plot; and 'Fable' (the word used by the older critics, up to the eighteenth century) does not at first sight suggest that meaning. But there is a very simple sense in which a Greek tragedy existed for the sake of the myth or Fable. With rare exceptions these tragedies were concerned with the great legends of Hellenic mythology: the counterpart of such Hebrew stories as those of Abraham, Moses, Samson, or Jezebel. And in legends of that sort, even when they are moral and exemplary, human character is subordinate to divine power: the story exists for the sake of what happens rather than as a study in human psychology. True, the characters are important—Aristotle ranks them second to the Fable; but they are secondary. Character, together with Intelligence, is the *natural* cause of what happens, and the success or failure of the persons in the story depends on it. But their fate is outside their control, and it is their fate (what happens) that determines their felicity or otherwise. Behind this argument lies a view of life so different from that of Christianity that we cannot accept it without question. Moreover, it postulates a subject matter peculiar to tragedy. It is obviously absurd to apply what Aristotle says to, say, *As You Like it*, or *She Stoops to Conquer*, or *Pride and Prejudice*.

There is, however, another line of argument discernible in Aristotle's analysis. The Fable is the presentation of the whole story; the Character or Intelligence of any person participating in it, however prominently, is only a part. There is a sense in which the whole of any work of art is invariably more important than the parts. Even supposing a play or novel consisted entirely of characters without any 'story' in the ordinary sense of the word, the synthesis of the characters might be held to be more important than any one of them, or indeed than the sum total of them all. In that sense, plot (there is no longer any need to fight shy of the word) would be more important than character. But, if it is so, the concept of plot must not be a rigid one: there are other ways of synthesising the elements of a story than to fit them into a logical sequence leading by a chain of cause and effect to an inevitable conclusion. Indeed, in many well-constructed comedies (for example, *As You Like It*, or *Tom Jones*) the conclusion is far from inevitable. It may be appropriate; but that is quite another matter.

In his Preface to Shakespeare, Dr Johnson remarked that 'Shakespeare's plays are not in the rigorous or critical sense either tragedies or comedies'. In saying that, Dr Johnson did not intend to find fault with Shakespeare, as his namesake Ben Jonson had done, for 'wanting art'. He was following a later tradition, begun by Dryden; he was praising Shakespeare as an irregular genius, a poet of nature, who understood life so profoundly that he could afford to defy the narrower proprieties of art. Dryden and Johnson were right in refusing to throw Shakespeare overboard because he did not satisfy the rigid notions of characterisation and plot that prevailed in the dramatic theory of their time. But it is no longer necessary to defend Shakespeare against that particular charge. Even Dryden (in his bolder moments), and Johnson (more consistently), suggested that it was the theory rather than Shakespeare that was wide of the mark. The fact is that the wholesale censure of Shakespeare's comic plots was not only 'rigorous' but *un*critical, since it was based on an unscientific application to comedy of Aristotle's theory of tragic drama. At least three of Shakespeare's comedies—*A Midsummer Night's Dream, As You Like It,* and *The Tempest*—are admirably plotted: because their structure or form follows a pattern appropriate to comedy, and *therefore* different from the Aristotelian pattern for tragedy.

But there seems no reason why we should not apply Aristotle's *method* to comic fiction, and first (in order to clear the air) to fiction in general. He himself discusses fiction at the beginning of the *Poetics:* and I believe that his argument is sound and that his conclusions are still in the main valid, though he gives his views so summarily that they are not easy to follow. His main conclusion is that fiction is essentially philosophical; that is what distinguishes it from fact, and actually makes it more important than fact. But perhaps it will be better to leave Aristotle, and ask over again the question: What is the end of fiction? What human need is satisfied by the telling of stories?

We cannot get a conclusive answer to this question from history. Most of the traditional forms of fiction—allegory, fable, parable, and myth—are didactic in purpose. They exist in order to tell people about life, not merely or even mainly to entertain idle minds by occupying them with exciting or agreeable fantasies; it is their didactic purpose that gives them their form. Sometimes they interpret in dramatic symbol the working of natural forces, as the myth of Cupid and his bow and arrows represent in a kind of metaphor the sudden and unexpected upsets that love causes in the human mind or body. Folk tales, like the Brer Rabbit stories, are more realistic; but they still owe their main interest to the shrewd psychology at the centre of each story. Myth and fable teach; parable and allegory more often, though not always, preach. But why did this indirect method of giving instruction ever come into being? There are two fairly obvious answers to this question, both of which at different times have been widely accepted as valid. The simple explanation is that the story form is used in order to gild the pill of instruction by giving amusement or excitement to the reader or listener as a kind of bribe. The other is that by using this form it is possible to go deeper than the reasoning intellect, and awaken feelings and sympathies, bringing the imagination of the listener into activity; so that he not merely knows and understands, but sees and feels. These two answers are superficially similar; but the difference between them is fundamental. And history cannot tell us whether the story is a by-product of the moral, or the moral of the story; it is a philosophical question, and perhaps we can only answer it by intuition.

Mr E. M. Forster maintains, perhaps with some irony, that it is the moral that is secondary. In *Aspects of the Novel* he draws a picture, based ostensibly on anthropology, but really of course on what he supposes to be the psychology of the modern reader.

Neanderthal man listened to stories, if one may judge by the shape of his skull. The primitive audience was an audience of shock-heads, gaping round the camp-fire, fatigued with contending against the mammoth or the hairy rhinoceros, and only kept awake by suspense. What would happen next? The novelist droned on, and as soon as the audience guessed what happened next, they either fell asleep or killed him.

It is hard to dispute Mr Forster's definition of a story as 'a narrative of events arranged in their time sequence'; and easy to take his next step, and conclude that 'it can have only one merit: that of making the audience want to know what happens next'. But to argue from a definition is always dangerous. One must first be sure that the definition is complete; that it does not leave out something essential.

Character and plot

Suppose I were to stand on a platform in Liverpool Street Station and record the things I saw happening in any given hour: unless I was very lucky, or unless I established an imaginary connexion between the separate happenings, the record would not be a story in the ordinary sense of the word. Or, to look at it from another point of view, is the appeal of stories merely to curiosity? Why does a good story improve even after repeated hearings? Everyone knows that children like stories. If this were merely out of curiosity they would want a new story every time, and preferably a new kind of story. But if one is to generalise, the truth is rather the opposite. Most children stick to one or two special stories until they have worn them out: Red Indian stories, or animal stories, or stories about princesses, or whatever it may be. What is more, they like nothing so much as to hear the same story over and over again; and if you vary it in any detail, so far from being pleased, they will correct you, usually with some annoyance. This behaviour of children seems to me an important clue to the character of fiction.

A small child's mind is insecure; unexpected things are always happening round him. He notices, however, that his elders know what is coming much more than he does: partly because they can make it come, and partly because they see patterns which are invisible to his restricted range of vision. The child therefore wants to be admitted, not into a world of surprises (he gets surprises enough in his daily life), but into a magically stable world, where things can be foretold and where they proceed according to plan. So also with primitive peoples. In folk-tales, and in the old ballads, the same incidents occur again and again in different stories. Moreover, both in the ballads and in children's stories, the incidents often fall into a pattern, as in the famous story of the Three Bears.

I suggest, therefore, that the essential cause of the popularity of fiction is not that it appeals to curiosity, but that it takes us for a time out of the haphazard, untidy, pointless world in which we live, into a world where things happen according to plan; that the appeal of fiction consists in pattern, order, and convention. Mr Forster's definition should be amended: 'a *significant* narrative'; and while we are amending it, we had better alter the second half to 'of a sequence of events', for the events are not always related in the order in which they are supposed to have occurred. Of course there are other appeals, too. Some people, who have got tired of routine or comfort, like stories that make their flesh creep. Others like stories where everyone is very kind and beautiful, or very brave and clever; or where fortune showers down wealth on a hero who started life with a small income or no income at all. Other people, not necessarily any cleverer, prefer stories where the characters are unpleasant, or where everything goes wrong. But these are personal preferences, and it is unscientific to generalise from them. We are on safer ground in assuming that the aim of every novelist, and the end of every novel, is to present to our imagination an artificial world, with a character of its own, depending on the mentality of the writer and in particular on his attitude to life. The meaning of a novel lies in the character of the world created by the writer: not merely, for example, in the character of the hero, or in the way the events are made to work out, though both of these are important factors and obviously help to determine the meaning. And the value of the novel depends on the quality of that created world. It must be more consistent than any average slice of life appears on the surface to be; but mere tidiness has little or no value. The order must be related to some end, particular or general, and it must also fit the material the artist is manipulating; just as in real life good discipline has to be based not only on an end in view but also on the natures of the people for whom it is intended.

The material of a work of fiction is not (as might at first sight appear) people, places, and events; it is not even life in general. It is ideas: ideas of people, ideas of places, ideas of events. That does not mean that a novelist is merely expressing his fancies or feelings. An idea is not purely subjective; it is a mental effort to assimilate something outside oneself, or conversely to put one's thoughts into the form of realities. The value of an idea depends therefore on three things: on the vitality (or, as we sometimes say, originality) of the mind of its creator, on his powers of observation, and lastly on his ability to adapt his mind to what he observes. Again, the test of an idea is not its accuracy: its closeness in all respects to the object to which it is attached. The process of perceiving an object or an event is much more complicated than we are apt to realise. The brains that perceive are not uniform, or empty, or passive at the time of perception; and the variation between our different ideas of any single object is of course slight

Character and plot

compared with the variation between our ideas of life in general. It is fair to conclude that no two painters looking at the same tree would have the same image of it; and *a fortiori* that no two persons have ever had the same idea of life. For an idea differs in function from a scientific observation. The scientific observer is under a strict and almost sacred obligation not to allow his notions of what things should be, or even of what they are, to affect his observations; and he uses instruments as far as possible, both to make and to record his observations for him. But the philosopher and the artist, who deal in ideas, have a more complicated (though not necessarily more difficult) task. On the one hand they have to make themselves into their own instruments, so that their perceptions are as sensitive and complete as is humanly possible, recording the smallest significant detail; but on the other hand, they put the whole of their knowledge and experience into the idea, so that what their knowledge and experience tells them is accidental or inessential or transient is modified or eliminated, and replaced by an image of the permanent essential nature of the object. The simplest kind of idea is a generalisation; a generalisation is an idea, because to form it one has not merely to make, but to co-ordinate, observations. Paradoxically, ideas of particular objects are more complicated than general ideas, because they are modified by all the general ideas relevant to the object; for this reason the artist (if he is left to himself) prefers the particular to the general, because it gives him richer ideas. This explains the natural predilection of artists for fiction: for particular scenes, particular events, and particular persons.

We can never, therefore, judge a work of fiction simply by whether it agrees with our own view, or even knowledge, of life: not only is that an injustice to the artist, but it deprives us of the very benefit that fiction exists to confer. For to censure a novel for its novelty is surely illogical. The only entirely satisfactory test of an idea or a compound of ideas (a work of art or philosophy) is its power to survive and to spread; reluctance to judge a new work of art is, therefore, not always cowardly—it may spring from wisdom and knowledge. Above all, it shows a lack of understanding to criticise any particular novelist, or novelists as a whole, because the persons they depict are 'unlike life'; for what we really mean by that is 'unlike our beliefs or notions about life', which are of course not the same thing as life itself. And it is a similar mistake to judge any story because it seems to be composed differently from our notions of the way life is composed. Most readers make this mistake in one form or another in judging the plot and characterisation of any work of fiction.

The greater part of what I have said about art is equally true of ethics. The world of ethics is also a world of ideas, modifying nature according to an artificial pattern. A moral man is a man who organises his conduct strictly according to his idea of life; and anyone who fails to do so is immoral. But for everyone to have an entirely different pattern of conduct would be inconvenient, not to say barbarous. Being by nature social, man is also conventional; he accepts a common view of life generally current in the society in which he lives, and with it a common pattern of behaviour. He is willing to do this in the interest of intelligibility and confidence. To be valid, these moral systems should embody a high (if possible, the highest) common factor of human knowledge and experience; but precisely because it is a common factor it can never lead to complete standardisation of behaviour. Within the convention, every man has to form his own idea of life and develop his personal pattern of conduct; and it is a curious fact that the more civilised a society is the simpler its ethic becomes, and the greater the freedom and responsibility of the individual. There is, however, a point beyond which latitude leads to decadence and anarchy, and so back to barbarism; and then humanity has to begin the process anew.

Conventions in literature develop side by side with ethical conventions; they are not the same, since the purpose of art is not identical with that of ethics, but they are allied. And in art, as in ethics, they are at first complicated and rigid; as confidence and intelligibility increase, they become simpler and leave greater freedom and responsibility to the individual; but if any people breaks away altogether from traditional modes and techniques, its literature will lose the social character that is a necessary condition of healthy art. In my first two chapters I tried to explain the general significance of the most important of the literary conventions, tragedy and comedy: tragedy, as an expression of the natural pride of man, defending himself as a sentient being with a will and convictions of his own against all the forces, human and superhuman, and inhuman, that fight against him; and comedy as an expression of the natural modesty of man, mixing with his kind, and defending them and himself against megalomania, egoism, misanthropy, and the

Character and plot 105

other forces of disintegration inside human nature. It is in the light of these ends that I must judge the traditional patterns of character and incident in comedy and tragedy.

II

To begin with, the characters are not real people; art is not a substitute for life. The artist is not even trying to give us real people, but to give us his idea of people; and if he is a comic artist, his idea of one particular aspect of people.

Tragic characters are isolated; and they tend to be either superhuman or subhuman. At the same time, although character is usually thus exaggerated in tragedy, it must always retain its fundamental humanity, or it will be melodramatic rather than tragic: as, for example, Barabas is in Marlowe's *Jew of Malta*. As Aristotle pointed out, a tragic character should not be either completely good or completely bad. We need to be able to identify ourselves with him, to imagine ourselves in his position, to sympathise with him; and a normal spectator cannot sympathise with complete goodness or badness. Lastly, the faults of a tragic character must not be the most important thing about him; if they are we shall be more conscious of his abnormality than of his humanity, and we shall tend to judge him. This is most destructive of the tragic effect. I have called attention to the tact with which Shakespeare keeps us out of a censorious mood towards Macbeth and Lear.

To be comic, on the other hand, a character must be seen as one unit in a society composed of other similar units; and he is judged according to the manners of his peers, or the science of psychology or the laws of morality. The characters of comedy are not superhuman or subhuman, but on a level with the generality of mankind; and if they are eccentric their eccentricity is regarded as sheer misfortune, like a disease. This is true even of the grandiose characters of comedy, like Shylock or Falstaff, or Volpone, or Sir Epicure Mammon. Perhaps indeed, Shylock and Falstaff should not be classed as comic characters. I am not sure that *The Merchant of Venice* is strictly speaking a comedy; certainly *Henry IV* is not. Probably one should not count a character as comic unless he occurs in a comedy, even if he has most of the characteristics of comic characters; since it is only in relation to a total effect that any

D*

of the elements in a work of fiction are either comic or tragic. But, to waive this possibly somewhat pedantic point, Shakespeare has been accused of awakening too much sympathy for Shylock or Falstaff, so that they become tragic. I am apt to think this is a sentimentalism, from which Shakespeare's contemporaries would have been free; but the very fact that the feeling exists confirms the general principle, that a comic character must not finally seem to us heroic, and that it must as a whole invite critical judgment rather than arouse strongly sympathetic feeling. I would add that it should not arouse a too strongly antipathetic feeling either: this suggests a main distinction between comedy and satire.

It was Ben Jonson's especial work to found a tradition for treating character in comic drama. Not that he was the first English writer who understood how to draw comic characters: more than two centuries earlier Chaucer had understood it at least as well, and performed it even better. But it was Jonson who hit on a formula that is still useful after nearly three hundred and fifty years. I will therefore say something at length about his ideas and his plays; for his plays are to a great extent controlled by his theories.

He was a wholehearted adherent of the new philosophy preached by Bacon at that turning point in our history when the Stuart dynasty succeeded the Tudor, and modern England may be said to have begun. He had two main ideas about comedy, both of them Baconian; one negative in tendency and on the whole deleterious, the other positive and very fruitful. The negative idea was that drama should adhere closely to nature: that it should give an accurate picture of the material world, based on knowledge and observation. Jonson rightly considered the average Elizabethan play both slovenly and over-sensational. His strictures on Shakespeare's art are well known, and have not been good for his own reputation; though I would plead in his defence that his tributes to Shakespeare are both just and generous, and that it has in the end been to Shakespeare's advantage that the other dramatic giant of his day resisted his influence. The most important of Jonson's criticisms of Shakespeare is the one in the Induction to *Bartholomew Fair*:

If there be never a servant-monster i' the Fair, who can help it, he [i.e. Jonson] says, nor a nest of anticks? He is loth to make Nature afraid in his plays, like those that beget *Tales, Tempests,* and suchlike drolleries. . . .

Character and plot

—an unmistakable allusion to *The Winter's Tale* and *The Tempest*. But Jonson's attack was directed rather against the general practice of his contemporaries and the theatrical customs of the time, than against Shakespeare in particular. The gist of it is contained in the Prologue to *Everyman in his Humour*, which is an important manifesto: I will therefore quote it in full.

> Though need make many poets, and some such
> As art and nature have not bettered much,
> Yet ours, for want, hath not so loved the stage
> As he dare serve the ill customs of the age,
> Or purchase your delight at such a rate
> As, for it, he himself must justly hate:
> To make a child, now swaddled, to proceed
> Man, and then shoot up, in one beard and weed,
> Past threescore years; or, with three rusty swords,
> And help of some few foot-and-half-foot words,
> Fight over York and Lancaster's long jars,
> And in the tiring-house bring wounds to scars:
> He rather prays you will be pleased to see
> One such today as other plays should be;
> Where neither chorus wafts you o'er the seas,
> Nor creaking throne comes down, the boys to please,
> Nor nimble squib is seen, to make afeared
> The gentlewomen, nor roll'd bullet heard,
> To say it thunders, nor tempestuous drum
> Rumbles, to tell you when the storm doth come;
> But deeds and language such as men do use,
> And persons such as Comedy would choose
> When she would show an image of the times
> And sport with human follies, not with crimes—
> Except we make 'em such, by loving still
> Our popular errors when we know they're ill,
> I mean such errors as you'll all confess,
> By laughing at them, they deserve no less:
> Which, when you heartily do, there's hope left then,
> You, that have so graced monsters, may like men.

He complains that the theatre is unrealistic; and that it is sensational, both in its machinery and in the characters themselves. On the other hand he professes to educate his audience away from fantasy and towards fact: from monsters to men.

As I have said, this realistic doctrine rests on a fallacy: that the material of which fiction is composed is real persons and events, which it can never be, and which it can only ruin itself by attempting to be. Fortunately Jonson did not even attempt to be completely realistic in his own plays. There is, however, some value in his insistence on *psychological* realism, for it is truly important that the characters of comedy should behave as people behave to one another; indeed both Titania and Caliban do so, though the one is a fairy and the other a monster. But the chief effect of this part of Jonson's propaganda concerns the previous chapter rather than this one; it did much to banish poetry from the English stage, and particularly the high poetical comedy in which Shakespeare excelled. Jonson's own style (like Wordsworth's) is often much better than the 'language really used by men'; but though it is vigorous, meaty, and often very amusing, it is neither graceful nor lucid. This is all the more to be regretted since Jonson was a poet and could write gracefully. However, it must be said that realism would have overtaken the English stage sooner or later, whether Jonson had advocated it or not: it was part of the larger materialistic tendency from which we have not yet emancipated ourselves. It is not in this that Jonson's importance lies.

What is important is his application to comedy of the psychological theory of humours. Neither the word nor the notion was invented by Jonson; it belonged to medieval medical theory, and in the burst of popular psychology about the end of the sixteenth century it had become a jargon word, very much as the word 'complex' did in the early twentieth century. Just as ignorant people a few years ago, if they wanted to sound impressive, explained every kind of behaviour by labelling it a complex, so in Jonson's day they used the word 'humour'. Jonson began by ridiculing this habit, as one of the follies of the time: in *Everyman in his Humour* it is defined as 'a gentlemanlike monster, bred in the special gallantry of our time by affectation, and fed by folly'. But he soon discovered that he had struck a vein invaluable for comedy; and in the Introduction to his next play, *Everyman out of his Humour*, he treats the word not as a mere affectation of speech, but as a name for something real and deep-seated in character.

> Why, humour (as 'tis *ens*) we thus define it:
> To be a quality of air or water,
> And in itself holds these two properties,

Character and plot

> Moisture and fluxure: as, for demonstration,
> Pour water on this floor, 'twill wet and run;
> Likewise the air, forced through a horn or trumpet,
> Flows instantly away and leaves behind
> A kind of dew; and hence we do conclude
> That whatsoe'er hath fluxure and humidity
> As wanting power to contain itself
> Is humour. So in every human body
> The choler, melancholy, phlegm, and blood,
> By reason that they flow continually
> In some one part, and are not continent,
> Receive the name of humours. *Now thus far*
> *It may by metaphor apply itself*
> *Unto the general disposition:*
> *As when some one peculiar quality*
> *Doth so possess a man that it doth draw*
> *All his affects, his spirits, and his powers,*
> *In their confluxions, all to run one way,*
> *This may be truly said to be a humour.*
> But that a rook, in wearing a pied feather,
> The cable hatband, or the three-piled ruff,
> A yard of shoe-tie, or the Switzer's knot
> On his French garters, should affect a humour,
> Oh, 'tis more than most ridiculous.

This notion is like the notion of the 'ruling passion' in early eighteenth-century philosophy; though Pope, for example, in the *Essay on Man*, rather naïvely assumes that everyone is thus ruled by one particular passion, which distorts his character. Jonson makes no such assumption: his 'humorous' characters are strictly eccentric, and so far *in*human. It is very much what we mean by an obsession.

It matters very little whether Jonson was converted to the idea as a scientific theory of character; what is important is his perception of its value for comedy, and that he made it a part of his dramatic technique. For this very simple recipe, as one may call it: that if you measure a collection of human eccentricities against each other you get comedy—is a discovery of what comedy had been trying to do all the time, and what at its best (in Aristophanes as well as in Chaucer and Shakespeare; in *The Frogs*, in *The Canterbury Tales*, in *A Midsummer Night's Dream*) it had been doing. And it also gave definition to comedy on one side (the side of characterisation) for the future; it is followed by Congreve and Fielding and Sterne and Goldsmith and Jane Austen and Meredith and Shaw. A somewhat confusing distinction between Comedy of Humours and Comedy of Manners has been introduced into the history of drama. The Comedy of Manners in England is generally supposed to have begun with Restoration drama; that is to say, in a period when the interest of educated Englishmen in metaphysics and ethics had begun to decline and psychology was usurping their place. But the evolution of literary modes is not so neatly chronological; a much earlier dramatist, Fletcher, is far more clearly in this class than either Wycherley or Congreve; and later still Fielding wrote Comedy of Humours in his novels and Goldsmith made a point of doing so in his plays. The term 'Manners' is itself rather misleading, for in the Seventeenth and Eighteenth Centuries it covered not merely outward conventions of behaviour, but character as revealed in conduct. If there is any difference between the two kinds it is that in the Comedy of Manners the dramatist concerns himself, more superficially, with behaviour rather than with the character underlying the behaviour; that he fixes his norm by convention rather than by psychology or ethics, and that his comedy is therefore narrower in significance—referred to the standards of a group of people in a particular time and place rather than to permanent and universal scientific or philosophical principles. The Comedy of Manners therefore at its best and most significant and most interesting turns into a Comedy of Humours.

Jonson's grasp of the nature of characterisation in comedy is also important in the history of literary criticism; for it enabled him to raise comedy to the level of a serious art-form, essentially different in aim and character from tragedy, but not inferior. For if tragedy is the bulwark of human self-respect against the pressure of circumstances, comedy is the weapon of man as a social being against defeatism and anarchy. That is the significance of the Comedy of Humours.

It is often said that the Comedy of Humours is by nature unimaginative: that it classifies people into types and invents appropriate speeches and actions for them, but never brings them to life—that is to say, it does not conceive them as complete human beings. There is something in this charge; Jonson seems to have regarded literature as a descriptive science. His characters do not often give us the kind of surprise that living people give us, and that we get also from almost all Shakespeare's greatest comic characters—for instance, Bottom, and Touchstone, and Benedick. That kind of surprise is to be distinguished from the carefully planned and worked-out surprise sprung on the reader usually in the last chapter or act, as in Jonson's *Epicœne* or Fielding's *Tom Jones*: which is purely artificial, and gives us no pleasure beyond the (considerable) pleasure of witnessing a display of skill and ingenuity on the part of the author. *Epicœne* has been much admired as an example of dramaturgy, and it was singled out by Dryden for special praise; but though it goes well on the stage it is not remarkable for its humours, and its characters are not interesting. But the Comedy of Humours does not exclude imagination; and Jonson's own imagination, though sluggish, was powerful like a heavy gun, when he allowed himself to bring it into action. This he did in *Volpone*, which gives the impression of having issued complete from Jonson's mind, rather than having been carefully put together like *Epicœne*. *Volpone* is remarkable in that it has not several humours, but a single humour—greed. No doubt Jonson's conscious aim was to classify as far as he could in a single play the chief varieties of avarice: the vice that the Jacobean moralists singled out as the worst and most characteristic evil of the day. The minor characters are no more than theatrical types—for the most part mere examples of avaricious depravity; they are deliberately presented like puppets or dummies. But this is appropriate, for that is what they are: not only according to the plot, where they are worked by Mosca and Volpone as though on strings, but, more generally speaking, as robbed of sense and feeling by their greed. But the hero gives us the true surprise of the imagination, as Shakespeare's characters do; not only by making a fool of himself over the virtuous and uninteresting Celia, but by his conduct at the end of the play. He is a grander miscreant than the others, but also a more human character; he is not devitalised by his vice. His greed is not so much for money, as for excitement. He cares more for the game he is playing than for its profits; so that when Mosca betrays him he chooses to lose his property and go to prison rather than let a common clever rogue who has been his dependant blackmail him with impunity. But the play is not a tragedy, or an uneasy half-tragedy; it is a triumph of what Jonson called 'art'. Volpone's last speech ('This is called mortifying of a fox') keeps the tone of the play uniform right up to the end. This is a comic tact, corresponding to the tact with which

Shakespeare preserves our sympathy with his heroes. Volpone neither needs nor receives sympathy.

But neither *Volpone* nor *Epicœne* is quite typical of Jonson. Probably his best known play is *Everyman in his Humour*, I suppose because of its title: but it is immature and comparatively dull. The plays most characteristic of his dramatic genius are *The Alchemist* and *Bartholomew Fair*. The themes of both plays are extremely simple. In *The Alchemist* three rogues (Face, Subtle, and Doll Common) set up a swindling establishment, where they make money out of a succession of fools and simpletons, until Face outwits the other two and so ends the play; and in *Bartholomew Fair* a number of witless and self-important citizens pass through the hands of the light-fingered and sharp-witted folk of the fair and suffer such misfortune as their varying weaknesses of head expose them to. This London underworld is the right setting for Jonson, and out of it he makes a world not so balanced and comprehensive as Shakespeare's but quite unique. No other dramatist so naturally combines the exuberance of the Elizabethan age with the good sense beloved of the eighteenth century. *Bartholomew Fair* is remarkable for its variety of characters, and Jonson handles them with the ease of a master. There is scarcely a dull moment from beginning to end; no English play comes anywhere near it for the unification of sheer quantity of material. *The Alchemist* cannot; but it contains Sir Epicure Mammon, who is Jonson's greatest character after Volpone. His huge speech when he is day-dreaming about the joys that alchemy will bring him, shows what Jonson's imagination could do, building on a quite commonplace humour. It is too long to quote in full: here are some extracts from it.

         I do mean
To have a list of wives and concubines
Equal with Solomon, who had the stone
Alike with me: and I will make me a back
With the elixir, that shall be as tough
As Hercules, to encounter fifty a night. . . .
I will have all my beds blown up, not stuffed;
Down is too hard. And then, mine oval room,
Filled with such pictures as Tiberius took
From Elephantis, and dull Aretine
But coldly imitated. Then, my glasses,
Cut in more subtle angles, to disperse

Character and plot

> And multiply the figures as I walk
> Naked between my succubae. My mists
> I'll have of perfume, vapoured 'bout the room,
> To lose ourselves in; and my baths, like pits,
> To fall into: from whence we will come forth
> And roll us dry in gossamer and roses. . . .
> The few that would give out themselves to be
> Court and town stallions, and each-where belie
> Ladies who are known most innocent, for them,
> Those will I beg to make me eunuchs of:
> And they shall fan me with ten estrich-tails
> Apiece, made in a plume, to gather wind.
> We will be brave, Puff, now we ha' the medicine.
> My meat shall all come in in Indian shells,
> Dishes of agate set in gold, and studded
> With emeralds, sapphires, hyacinths and rubies. . . .
> My foot-boy shall eat pheasants, calvered salmons,
> Knots, godwits, lampreys: I myself will have
> The beards of barbles served instead of salads,
> Oiled mushrooms, and the swelling unctuous paps
> Of a fat pregnant sow, newly cut off,
> Dressed with an exquisite and poignant sauce;
> For which I'll say unto my cook 'There's gold
> Go forth, and be a knight'. . . .

Perhaps that is enough. Jonson did not know as well as Chaucer when to stop; but there is little of Sir Epicure that one would willingly lose.

These two plays are free from Jonson's besetting weakness: preaching. They are not directly didactic; Jonson is at last really content to sport with follies. It is not the virtuous man, but the resourceful and clever man, who prospers in them. They are not, as is sometimes supposed, satires upon rogues and swindlers; they are studies in the folly of their victims. This is not only better comedy, but also far better morality than the morality of 'poetic justice'. And it suggests an important principle of comic characterisation: that in comedy character consists not so much in goodness or wickedness as in efficiency or inefficiency: in courage or cowardice, cleverness or stupidity, good sense or folly. This does not mean that the hero of a comedy cannot be virtuous, but only that he is a comic hero not because of virtue, but because of his good sense. The principle is not obvious, since comedy is the natural ally of morality;

but the best comedy leaves the moral to be drawn by the spectator. It is the chief weakness of the later sentimental 'comedy' that it does not do so.

The typical Jonsonian comic character is one of a crowd; Volpone is exceptional. Even the magniloquent Sir Epicure is a mere dupe of Face and Subtle. That is the nature of the Comedy of Humours. Chaucer's Canterbury pilgrimage has no hero; nor has *Troilus and Criseyde*—the three main characters are all of equal importance in the action. Indeed it is a main aim of all comedy to stress the unheroic element in life, and this naturally affects the pattern appropriate to it, especially its characterisation and plot.

The most distinguished later dramatist of Humours is Goldsmith. In his best work he was inspired, like Fielding, by amused disgust with a kind of fiction that seemed to him both unhealthy and ridiculous. In the preface to *The Good-Natured Man* he complains of the gentility of the stage, and says that he wants to get back to 'nature and humour', which had been the foundations of the comedy of the last age. His plays were thus a palpable attack on sentimental comedy. It is not emotion that Goldsmith objects to, but false emotion. He himself had a genuinely soft heart—too soft; he did not need theatrical situations to move him to tears. But if his heart was soft, his brain was shrewd. *The Good-Natured Man* is a study in a certain sort of egoism: the desire for popularity and dislike of giving offence, which leads in the end to complete loss of personality, the inability to assert oneself or do anything positive, so that one is useless not only to oneself but to everyone else. *She Stoops to Conquer* is not so serious; but again it is based on a humour —that form of conceited timidity which makes a man flirt with barmaids, while he runs away from women who are his social equals.

Goldsmith is nearly one of the greatest English dramatists; it is surprising that he only wrote two plays, and that one of them is marred by a weak and unconvincing end. *The Good-Natured Man* has an excellent theme, which has never so far as I know been tackled by any other English dramatist. Honeywood is in love with Miss Richland, and she is in love with him; but he will not court her because of his false modesty, which makes him think about himself all the time instead of thinking of her. Goldsmith makes Honeywood actually press the courtship of other men on his unwilling mistress; this may seem far-fetched, but it is true to human nature.

After all, however, Goldsmith had not the heart to carry the situation to its logical end; if he had been a Molière he would have punished Honeywood in the only appropriate way. Assuming that he was no good, Miss Richland should not have accepted him; for it is a principle of comedy that those who will not help themselves may not be helped by the dramatist. Alternatively, Goldsmith might have worked a real reformation in Honeywood's character: made him pull himself together and exercise a little cunning and ruthlessness to get the woman he loved, and enough *real* good nature to understand and respond to her love of him. Goldsmith does neither; for he could not bring himself to see through this false good nature altogether. No doubt he was caricaturing himself in his hero; and probably only morbid writers can depict their *serious* faults on the stage with complete conviction. Goldsmith wants us to feel that after all Honeywood really is rather nice, and that undermines the whole theme of the play, which is that he is a sham.

But *She Stoops to Conquer* is a complete success. Here Goldsmith's touch is throughout so light, and he is so tolerant and amusing, that we forget how unpleasant is the type to which Marlowe belongs. The moral is established without a shade of moral indignation, and the disease is cured without any bedside manner to insist what a dangerous disease it is.

Although I have said that it is the nature of the Comedy of Humours for its characters to be units in a crowd, the interest may be centred in a single person; as it is in *The Good-Natured Man* and in *Volpone*. Naturally this is not so common in drama as in the novel, where the writer has more space at his disposal, and more inducement to subordinate the lesser characters to the more important; but even in the novel interest is not always focussed on a single character. It is not so in *Tristram Shandy*: and although Tom Jones is most emphatically a hero, the significance of Fielding's novel lies rather in the contrast between Tom and Blifil than in Tom as an independent character-study. But in Jane Austen's novels there is always a central character; and her heroines deserve special attention.

The most successful of them are Catherine Morland, Elizabeth Bennet, Emma Woodhouse, and Anne Elliot. They are all on a different plane from the other characters, partly because the whole story is seen through their eyes, and partly because, in spite of the dualistic titles of some of Jane Austen's novels, they all primarily concern one character. Darcy and Mr Knightley and Captain

Wentworth also stand out, but they are seen almost entirely from the outside. This, as I have said, is the reason why they are often misjudged; the reader does not realise that he is sharing the somewhat distorted view of the heroine, like a reader of detective fiction picking up the wrong clue. Darcy is the most striking example of this.

The general formula for a Jane Austen heroine is a mind learning from experience; this is of course particularly true of Catherine, but it is true also of Elizabeth, Emma, and Anne. Even Anne, who has already repented of her mistake before the book begins, has still to overcome the diffidence that led to it: the painful self-consciousness of an intelligent but somewhat priggish nature. The development of character in these heroines is revealed mainly by means of that 'internal' comedy, of which I have given an example on pages 28–9, and in which Jane Austen excelled. In chapter 3, speaking of the subject matter of comedy, I wrote that since it is the main concern of the comic writer to discriminate between what is normal and abnormal in human behaviour, most of the characters he depicts must necessarily be abnormal: but 'the abnormality of comic characters is not absolute: we should feel that they are capable of behaving normally if they would'. It is when the will to behave normally is strong in a character that internal comedy becomes possible; and it is a feature of all Jane Austen's heroines that they have this will. Clearly, if comedy is to deal with efficient people as well as misfits, it must embrace a superior class of characters with the power of fruitful self-criticism; the most important virtues of comedy being courage, honesty, and disinterestedness.

These virtues are also characteristic of Jane Austen's heroes; but since Jane Austen shows them mainly in action, as they appear to Elizabeth or Emma or Anne, these heroines must have keen perceptions. They are noticing young women. This does not mean that their judgments are correct; on the contrary they are usually emphatic but faulty. For instance, Emma judges Mrs Elton correctly, but she misjudges almost every other character in the book except herself; and this makes her an excellent character for comedy—intelligent, honest, and lively, but rather conceited and very far from wise.

It is the social aspect of character, then, that is shown in comedy. The most considerable body of English comedy in which there is a strict convention as to character is Restoration Comedy. In these

Character and plot

plays there are two main criteria by which the characters are judged. The first is the distinction, clearly envisaged and constantly emphasised, between the 'fop' and the 'wit': the most important test of masculine character in that class and at that time. Manners and fashions have changed much since 1700, and the distinction is no longer as clear as it was; even Mirabell has been described as a fop! The difference between the two types is that the fop bases his whole life on fashion; whereas the wit conforms to convention so far as convention is convenient, but relies for guidance on his own experience and his brains. To the fop life is a ritual; to the wit it is part game, part battle. The other important distinction is between good nature and malice: this distinction is equally important in the male and in the female characters. It is what places Millamant (whose very malice is good-natured) and Mrs Marwood (whose actions are entirely motivated by spite) in two utterly different worlds; as also Fainall and Mirabell—the scene quoted on pages 89–90 reveals this very clearly.

These two criteria of conduct cover almost the whole field of character-values in comedy.

III

It might be better if we put the word 'plot' out of commission, and spoke on the one hand of *structure* or *design* (which is what plot really means) and on the other hand of the *story* (which is something quite different). When people speak of a plot, they usually have in mind a logical sequence of significant events, like the events that lead from the return of Oedipus to his native country up to the death of his wife and his own blindness, or from Macbeth's military successes to his murder of Duncan and on to his own death. With this notion in mind, critics find fault with a large proportion of our comedies: Shakespeare's comic plots are careless, Jane Austen's are trivial, Congreve's are improbable, Sterne's are non-existent. This is based on a fallacy: that the plot of a comedy ought to be of the same kind as that of a tragedy. But the end of comedy is not the same as the end of tragedy; and this not only justifies but demands a difference of structure.

One of Aristotle's most profound principles is his principle of 'probability or necessity' in a work of fiction. By this he does not mean that the writer must give us a picture of what has often happened and is therefore probable in a merely statistical sense; but rather that he must depict 'what would happen'. Unfortunately he does not finish the sentence by giving the 'if' clause. From what he says elsewhere in the *Poetics* we may conclude that he meant 'what would happen given the hypotheses on which the story is based'; or 'what is the right sort of thing to happen in a really consistent world'. In writing of tragedy he stresses chiefly the need for probability in the sequence of events. In this he was quite right. A feeling that the hero is doomed from the very beginning of the play stresses his loneliness and importance, throws the other characters into the shade, and so gives us a sense of the significance of the individual and his particular environment. Unless there is a logical sequence of cause and effect in the events from beginning to end, the tragic atmosphere is lost; and if chance or accident interferes with this sequence at a single point, the tragic atmosphere is so far disturbed. But this is not the effect at which comedy is aiming. For in comedy we must feel that man is free, not fated; if anything goes wrong with him, the remedy is in his own hands. Shakespeare and Jane Austen and the rest of them were therefore quite right not to do in comedy what Aristotle (also quite rightly) had said that the tragic dramatist should do. For to show the free interplay of character, you must release your men and women from the pressure of circumstance: you must therefore make your story either fantastic (as Shakespeare does) or commonplace (as Jane Austen does). A comedy may even fail in its effect simply because the author has taken pains to make the plot conform strictly to the law of cause and effect; because he has insisted too ruthlessly on fate, and especially retribution. *The Egoist* is an instance of this: if ever a character in fiction was irretrievably doomed from the very first chapter to fail of his ambitions and be stripped of self-respect, it is Sir Willoughby Patterne; and Meredith works out his doom with the utmost skill and almost uncanny insight into the logic of events, step by step to the destined end.

The pattern we want in comedy is of a different kind: a grouping of characters rather than a march of events. In comedy it is in the contrast and balance of characters that probability is concentrated and the imagination and originality of the writer is displayed. The finest comic plot I know is that of *Don Quixote,* where the whole significance of the story lies in the contrast between Quixote and

Sancho Panza, and in two subordinate contrasts within this dominant one: between Quixote's nobility of mind and his absurdity of behaviour, and between Sancho's cynical peasant selfishness and his irrational loyalty to his master. Not only does this book contain two of the most famous characters in the literature of the world; but in conceiving them Cervantes almost divided the whole of human nature in two, with the neatness of a surgeon's knife. Yet in *Don Quixote* it does not matter whether the events have any particular connexion with each other; it does not even matter what order they come in; and they are all trivial and mostly fantastic. What matters is that the characters become increasingly clear, both in their relationship to each other and as representatives of human nature.

For perfect design the nearest rival to *Don Quixote* in our literature is *Tristram Shandy*, with its finely balanced quartet of central characters—Walter and Toby Shandy, Yorick and Corporal Trim; but it has not the range and simplicity and greatness of conception that *Don Quixote* has. A similar balance of character marks the design of Shakespeare's best constructed comedies: *A Midsummer Night's Dream*, *As You Like It*, and *The Tempest*. In the first the lovers, the fairies, and the artisans, and in the last Prospero, Ariel, and Caliban, all present important aspects of life and relate them to one another; with greater gaiety in the early play and greater profundity in the late one. In *As You Like It* the differentiation between types is less bold, but the interplay is subtler. Duke Frederick, the banished Duke, Jaques, Rosalind, Touchstone, and Audrey form a chain, each link of which shows up the previous one, beginning with the most unnatural character and ending with the most unsophisticated. The plot is complete with Touchstone's famous saying, 'a poor virgin, sir, an ill-favoured thing, sir, *but mine own*', which is perhaps the wisest comment ever made by a great poet on human nature.

Of later plays the most Shakespearean in structure is Congreve's *Way of the World*. In spite of superficial differences, Congreve's dramatic technique resembles Shakespeare's. From the first he broke completely with the principles of probability and realism as they were understood and preached (one might almost say, *commanded*) by Ben Jonson. He was indifferent about minor details of the action, and shaped it as he went along, adding scene to scene for dramatic effect. I have elsewhere mentioned his use of soliloquies and asides, and his fantasy in the dramatisation of character. In *The Double-Dealer* alone he used a severer technique, deliberately, to discipline himself; the exercise was good for his art, but being based on the 'rigorous and critical' (or uncritical) idea of drama, it was neither congenial to him nor successful. In *The Way of the World* on the other hand, the story or 'intrigue' as it is sometimes called, is very complicated and obscure, as well as rather improbable: the manœuvres between Fainall and Mrs Marwood on the one side and Mirabell and Millamant on the other, with Lady Wishfort as the tool of each party in turn, are extremely difficult to follow. If we regard this intrigue as the plot of the play we may well complain that Congreve did not know his business as a dramatist. But if we take the intrigue on trust and concentrate on the grouping of characters, as we should always do in comedy, it is far otherwise. Congreve explains his purpose in the dedication of the play: 'to design some characters which shou'd appear ridiculous, not so much thro' a natural Folly (which is incorrigible, and therefore not proper for the stage) as thro' an affected wit; a wit, which at the same time that it is affected is also false'. His theme is affectation, in its full range—from the affectation of youth and beauty in the vulgar and decayed Lady Wishfort, and the deliberate dishonesty of Fainall, up to its highest point in Millamant, with her charming pretence of heartlessness and independence, which has already begun to break down at the beginning of the play. Against affectation Congreve sets nature, which includes *good* nature; and he distinguishes with great subtlety between those whose good nature is merely disguised and those whose nature is bad, rotten, corrupt; those in whom nature is marred by superficial faults, and those into whose nature dishonesty has eaten until it has killed it. I have mentioned the gradually increasing clearness with which Fainall and Mrs Marwood are contrasted with Mirabell and Millamant; and on a lower level the same purpose is served by the steady rise of Sir Wilful Witwoud in effectiveness and the steady fall of the fop his brother.

A good comic plot is evidence of clear-sightedness in the author. *The Way of the World* marks a great development in Congreve's own mind. He has himself finally abandoned the affectation of heartlessness which is a defect of much Restoration Comedy, and to some extent of his own earlier plays; and he has ceased to care deeply about cleverness. But this does not mean any falling off in brilliance. The moral is put forward with perfect art; without a trace of pomposity. Nor does he lose sight of his standards in a gushing up of naïve benevolence, as lesser writers sometimes do when they become 'serious'. He is merciless to Fainall, and even to poor Mrs Marwood; also to the less dangerous but equally poisonous Witwoud. On the other hand Lady Wishfort and Mrs Fainall, who are merely shallow and feckless, have to suffer for their weakness, but Congreve lets them down lightly in the end. The play is perfect in its humanity and sense of proportion. It has that sincerity which is so important in literature, but so hard to define or judge.

There is a somewhat similar contrast between the intrigue and the real plot in *Tom Jones*. Fielding has been praised for the skill with which he keeps the secret of Tom's parentage in the early part of the book and unravels it at the end; and it is plausible that the shock of believing Mrs Waters to have been his own mother should finally have cured Tom of promiscuous inflammability. But as a whole the story is very improbable; there are too many coincidences by half; and Tom owes his final good fortune scarcely at all to his own efforts and almost entirely to the good will of the author. Fielding professes throughout the book to be following nature: to be depicting life as it is, rather than as it ought to be. He keeps this promise pretty well in depicting his characters, especially his hero; but he cannot be said to do so in the events at the end of the story. The way everything is made suddenly to go right for Tom and wrong for Blifil is outrageous; even if we are prepared to grant that in this world dishonesty is usually detected in the end and virtue is upon the whole rewarded in pounds, shillings, and pence, we must boggle at the convenience and neatness with which justice does itself in this story.

Yet once we have grasped the real principle on which the book is constructed these criticisms become irrelevant. Fielding does not give us an inevitable development in the fortunes of Tom Jones, as for example Hardy does for Henchard in *The Mayor of Casterbridge*. The plot of *Tom Jones* is a comic plot, based on the grouping of the characters rather than on the sequence of events. The centre of the picture is the contrast between Tom and his half-brother Blifil; between man as a spontaneous animal, and man as a calculating machine. But that by itself would not say more than a quarter of what Fielding has to say. The book is not a defence of animalism, so Fielding gives us two more 'animals' to contrast with Tom, Squire Western and Molly Seagrim, the one deprived of his wits by coarse habits, and the other deprived of honesty and self-respect by her bad heredity and environment. They throw into further relief Tom's character, which is both sensitive and honest; and on the other side there is Sophia, who has Tom's naturalness without his faults. Again, in the Blifil camp there are two minor rascals, Thwackum and Square; they are as selfish and dishonest as he is, but they make him look blacker both because they lack his cool-headed cunning, and because they have some sort of principles; and they are themselves contrasted and receive different treatment in the end, for Square is at least free from the cruelty and ill-nature of Thwackum and Blifil. There is also the contrast of Sophia's liveliness and breeding with the rather corrupt liveliness of Mrs Fitzpatrick and the superficial breeding of Lady Bellaston; and yet another contrast between the selfish fecklessness of Partridge and the disinterested fecklessness of Tom. So one could go on: at the circumference there is the richest variety of contrast; but it always in one way or another illustrates the main theme, which stands out boldly and clearly in the centre.

In the best-plotted of Jane Austen's novels—*Emma*—there is no such contrast between plot and intrigue; nor is the grouping of the characters so obvious. Yet although we can trace a logical sequence of events leading up to the marriage of Emma and Mr Knightley, and although the crisis of this story (the scene I quoted in chapter 2) coincides with the crisis of the plot, the significance of the book clearly lies in how Emma's character develops and reveals itself, rather than in what happens to and around her. Character and incident are however much better co-ordinated than is usual in comedy. Jane Fairfax is Emma's main foil; she has more talent and depth of character than Emma, and quite involuntarily steals her thunder. She is moreover a tragic character; it was very bold of Jane Austen to introduce her into a comedy and even to set her tragedy in motion by tying her to the shallow and selfish Frank. The tragedy is not more than hinted and does not break through the comic microcosm of Highbury; but these two characters are not masters of their fate as Emma and Mr Knightley are. What they do to Emma is to develop, for a time, her meaner side, just as Mr Knightley more permanently and deeply brings out her better side. Somewhat similarly, as Miss Bates shows up the coarsest strain in Emma (much to Mr Knightley's distress), so Mrs Elton by contrast reveals Emma's fundamentally good breeding. I have already noted the irony by which the positions of Emma and Harriet are momentarily reversed at the crisis; there is a similar reversal of the positions of Mr Knightley and Emma, when Mr Knightley, who has put her in her place so firmly all her life, suddenly finds himself thrown off his balance, and even driven from the field, by jealousy of Frank.

The explanation of Jane Austen's sense of form in the novel lies in her understanding of character and her firm and well-tried ethical code; in these respects she far excels any English comic writer except Chaucer. One has to go back to *Troilus and Criseyde* to find any comedy so contrapuntal as *Emma*. The character and incident patterns can both be perceived separately, but they harmonise at every point, and together form a pattern in two dimensions.

But after all Chaucer is unsurpassed by any of his successors in the art of narrative. In *Troilus and Criseyde*, though it is a long poem, there are only five effective characters: Troilus, Criseyde, Pandarus, Diomede, and Hector. But there is another actor in the drama: public opinion, which plays an important part at two points. At the very beginning of the poem, when Criseyde's father Calkas has fled to the Greeks, the Trojans in their fury cry out for vengeance on him and his whole family; which drives Criseyde in great fear to seek Hector's protection. Again at the beginning of Book IV, when the Greeks have offered to exchange Antenor for Criseyde, Hector protests that she is not a prisoner and that Trojans do not sell women; but there is a fresh outcry of the people, to which the parliament yields, and Criseyde is in due course handed over. The stupidity and cruelty of popular feeling is one of Chaucer's persistent themes (for example it is the main theme of the *Clerk's Tale*, and calls forth the only comment in the whole of the *Canterbury Tales* that he makes in his own person). This hungry malice of the mob is the background of the story of Troilus and Criseyde; it is the only external force of any importance with which the main characters have to contend. It defeats Hector, upon whose abilities as a soldier and virtues as a man the fortunes of Troy depend; it completely silences Troilus on this occasion, though he is afterwards prepared to defy it by carrying Criseyde off; and Criseyde's fear of it is her strongest motive, outweighing both her love for Troilus and her self-respect.

If the pressure of public opinion were irresistible, the story would be what Chaucer calls it, a tragedy. But though he represents it as formidable, there is no reason to suppose that he regarded it as decisive, in this story at any rate. When Pandarus is trying to rouse Troilus from his despair one of his arguments is that public opinion is as ephemeral as it is violent.

> Pandare answerde, 'Freend, thow maist, for me
> Don as the list; but hadde ich it so hoote,
> And thyn estat, she sholde go with me,
> Though al this town cride on this thyng by note.
> I nolde sette at al that noys a grote!
> For whan men han wel cryd, than wol they rowne;
> Ek wonder last but nyne nyght nevere in towne.'

To be sure, Pandarus is not Chaucer's mouthpiece; he is a character in the story, with a point of view of his own, with which Chaucer in the end does not identify himself. But the plot in this instance confirms Pandarus's opinion; indeed Troilus decides to take his advice, and he would have done so but for Criseyde's resistance. Even despite it he would have carried her off at the last moment if he had not been afraid of hurting her in the scuffle.

For the rest, the story as Chaucer tells it, consists entirely of the interplay of character, with Criseyde's conduct as the main theme: her slippery heart, and how she 'falsed' Troilus. It might be argued that it was not her fault that Troilus fell in love with her, or that the Trojans decided to send her to her father in exchange for Antenor. And further, that she was tricked into yielding to Troilus, and he had no right to expect her to be faithful to him. But that is not how Chaucer feels, nor (perhaps more important still) how Criseyde herself feels. Chaucer says that he does not want to blame her, and that he would excuse her *if he could*: and he tells us that no woman ever grieved more than she did when she was false to Troilus. And this clear judgment on Criseyde's conduct is in the spirit of comedy rather than tragedy; for tragedy feels with fallen character and does not pass judgment on it. The truth is that for all her cautious hesitations she is glad enough to find herself in the arms of Troilus; indeed, with the frankness that is one of her good qualities she confesses that if she had not already yielded she would not be where she was. And after she has left Troilus for Diomede, she acquits him of all blame.

Yet we cannot altogether do so. We judge him for allowing Pandarus to do his wooing for him, and in such a way as to make Troilus's high-flown sentiments sound rather silly. Not that he is a

Character and plot

hypocrite; but he is in a completely false position, as false as Tom Jones's position when he pays court to Lady Bellaston for the sake of the money she gives him. And we also perhaps blame him for not understanding Criseyde, and so making an unfair demand on her good-natured but easy-going character.

Indeed, one cannot imagine anyone less suited to be his mistress than Criseyde was; and so, lastly, we judge Pandarus, who knew both of them well, but yielded, even more disastrously than Emma, to his taste for match-making. His intentions were no doubt good; but the searching standards of comedy take little account of good intentions. When Troilus and Criseyde are faced with their first real difficulty, we perceive what an ill friend he has been to both of them. We also remember (what Chaucer has told us more than once) that Pandarus had made a mess of his own love affairs; and we do not wonder that he has led them into an even worse mess. The utter inadequacy of his charming cynicism is completely shown up; he becomes increasingly futile and pathetic, and in the end he can do nothing but abuse Criseyde, which he of all people has no right to do, and which Troilus is too much of a man to do. The truth of Chaucer's imagination is shown in the way Pandarus thus fades out of the story in its final phase, although he has been easily the most effective and attractive character during the preliminaries. For Pandarus is neither a fool nor a knave; only, when he is placed in a group with Criseyde and Troilus, his deficiencies show up, at least to Chaucer's searching eye.

The crucial scene is the last talk of the two lovers in bed, on the night before Criseyde leaves Troy. Criseyde is very plausible. She must go, but she will come back. She will of course do what he tells her to do—but parliament has decided to send her to her father. It is a cruel pain to them—but it is only half a morning's ride away. There is a truce; he will hear her news, and before the truce is over she will be back. As it is, a fortnight has often passed between their meetings—can he not wait ten days for her now? All her kinsfolk except her father are in Troy; so is her property; so above all is her dear love. All her father wants is to know how she is faring in Troy; and when he knows that she is happy they need not fear that he will keep her. Besides, everyone is talking about peace. And even if there is no peace, what should she do in the Greek camp, in constant fear among all those soldiers? And her father is old; she will persuade him to send her back to fetch money, and to make his peace with Priam—she will convert him from his own oracles. So her spirits rise until she has recovered her usual gaiety, and Chaucer says she really meant it; and Troilus listens to the rigmarole, and though his heart misgives him he forces himself to trust her. But before he agrees, he tells her of his misgivings, and how it is not so easy and simple as she says, and begs her to steal away with him in the morning, before it is too late; he has friends who will receive them with honour. But Criseyde will not hear of it: they can steal away, but they will regret it if they do. His fears are all causeless. Troy needs his help. What will people say if they run away? What about his reputation, and hers? Troilus is still unconvinced. He can wait ten days: but he begs her for the love of God to steal away with him, for his heart tells him that is the best thing to do. And then she uses her last woman's weapon: 'I see you don't trust me—if you saw how it hurt me you wouldn't go on talking like that.' And she repeats her promise to return, and bids him cheer up and not make their last moments miserable—and to be true to her whatever happens. So he gives way, ending with a sad line 'I can na more, it shal be founde at preve.' And so, alas, it is.

On this scene of pathetic comedy all that has come before converges; and from it all that is to happen issues. The frivolity of Criseyde, talking herself out of difficulties too grave for mere talk; her overriding concern for respectability; her unscrupulous management of Troilus: for all these Chaucer has prepared us in the scene between Criseyde and Hector, the conversations between her and Pandarus, and the internal comedy of her hesitations before she gives herself to Troilus. But what comes as a shock in this scene is that Troilus plainly does not trust her. This is partly because he does not trust himself; he has never tested his hold over Criseyde, never even courted her himself—it has all been done by Pandarus. One is tempted to wish at this point that he had more of the Diomede in him, for Diomede is obviously the right sort of lover for Criseyde. But the wish involves a misunderstanding of the whole story. Criseyde is speaking the truth in two things that she says, out of all the welter of self-deception. She will do what Troilus orders her to do; that is in character. She has done what Pandarus wanted her to do, although she ought never to have involved herself with anyone so much in earnest as Troilus; and she is destined by her nature to do what Diomede wants her to do. And her other true saying is that if they go away together they will regret it. For though Troilus is prepared to give up everything for her, she is not prepared to give up her comforts and her respectability. And all this Troilus perceives in his heart, if not with his head. He knows that she is the wrong woman for him, and he is right to let her go: 'it shal be founde at preve'. It is too late to put Criseyde's love to the test (that should have been done before); but it is better to trust it than to keep her by force, and as an increasingly unwilling mistress. For Criseyde is not a girl, but a mature woman, with her character (such as it is) fully formed.

In the strange end of the poem Troilus looks down from heaven and laughs at the sorrow of those who are weeping over his death; and he passes judgment on 'the blynde lust, the which that may nat laste'. Some modern readers doubt the sincerity of Chaucer's exhortation to 'yonge fresshe folkes, he or she' to repair home to God from worldly vanity. But this is the moral of the poem, though a twentieth-century writer would probably have left God out of it; for truly the love-affair was not worth all the fuss and feeling that it caused. And it is well that Troilus should have the last laugh, rather than Pandarus; for he alone of the trio has enough character to learn the wisdom that can see things in their true proportion. True, he was a fool over Criseyde; but as Blake says, the fool who persists in his folly will become wise. True also that modern comedies do not as a rule end in heaven; but there is no reason why they should not (and Shaw's *St Joan* almost does). Besides, heaven was a more natural and real place to the fourteenth-century Englishman than to his descendant of the twentieth century. In any case, tragedies do not end in wise laughter.

In these sometimes rather lengthy analyses I have tried to illustrate the nature of plot in comedy. I have argued that a lack of logic in the sequence of events so far from being a weakness in the art of the writer, is proper in comedy; though provided the events are not in themselves out of the ordinary (as in *Emma* and *Troilus*) they may be made to follow a logical sequence. What is essential to a good comic plot is an exact balance and proportion between the characters, and a progressive revelation of their true nature by means of contrast, interplay, and mutual influence. Partly because of Aristotle, but without his authority (for he was writing of tragedy) the only kind of plot we are accustomed to recognise is a pattern in time. But there is no justification for this narrow view. There are at least two kinds of plot: the tragic plot, in *time*, and the comic plot, in *space*.

6

THE BOUNDARIES OF COMEDY

I

The chief difficulty in any attempt to discover the character of comedy by inductive methods is the selection of specimens from which to generalise; for we cannot make the selection without first forming a notion of comedy to guide us in making it. I began by putting forward an idea of comedy, and I have based my selection of specimens on that idea. I cannot therefore pretend to have used what in this century would be regarded as a strictly scientific method, nor do I think such a method is applicable to literature except within narrower limits and for narrower purposes than those of this book. Yet to begin with an idea and then clarify it by examples is not a disingenuous or improper approach to literature; on the contrary it is the only possible method of generalisation open to a literary critic. As I have said in an earlier chapter, ideas properly so called are not arbitrary; they are not formed in some isolated vacuum of the mind; they are the result of innumerable perceptions which the mind has assimilated, reconciled with such knowledge and experience as it possesses, and so clarified to the best of its ability. This no man can claim to do with absolute truth or validity; but he can hope to approximate by this method to the truth, and to be judged thereafter by results.

The idea of comedy that I took for my starting-point covers, and is derived from, a variety of authors of whom Chaucer, Shakespeare, Ben Jonson, Congreve, Goldsmith, Sterne, Fielding, Jane Austen, and Bernard Shaw are the chief. It is primarily an English idea of comedy; but not exclusively English, for not only Cervantes and Molière, but many modern French plays, and even

The boundaries of comedy

M. René Clair's films, have contributed to it. So also has much that has been written about comedy, from the time of Ben Jonson onwards; and also indirectly, much that has been written about other branches of drama and literature, and about literature generally. The frontiers of comedy have thus marked themselves out in my mind somewhat more clearly than the chances of variable and accidental nomenclature mark them out, and somewhat differently. Apart from this, I have tried to use an inductive method, and to allow my examples to speak for themselves. But since I have found myself including one important poem that has passed as a tragedy, and excluding some plays that have passed as comedies, it remains to say something of the frontier territory and what lies immediately beyond it.

In every respect—in subject matter, style, characterisation, and structure—tragedy parallels and contrasts with comedy. The contrast is so striking and significant that almost all writers from Aristotle onwards until quite recently have assumed that they are not mere conventions, but reflect real permanent truth. This conviction is neither strong nor generally accepted at the present time. It is true that there is nothing either tragic or comic but thinking makes it so. Yet if thinking makes it so, it is so; thinking is a reality. On the other hand, it is not always by any means easy to draw the line between tragedy and comedy, perhaps because the line is not artificial but natural. One source of this difficulty is custom, which plays tricks with nomenclature to the embarrassment of philosophers. Chaucer called *Troilus and Criseyde* his 'litel tragedye', and it is unthinkable that so great and careful a writer should have blundered in thus describing the best planned and most clearly envisaged of all his stories. By great good fortune, however, he has himself given a definition in some well-known lines in the prologue to the *Monk's Tale*, which show that the medieval idea of tragedy did not exactly tally with that of either ancient Greece or modern Europe; it selects a common feature of tragedy, but a feature that is neither absolutely essential to tragedy, nor entirely inconsistent with comedy.

> Tragedie is to seyn a certein storie,
> As olde bookes maken us memorie,
> Of hym that stood in greet prosperitee,
> And is yfallen out of heigh degree
> Into myserie, and endeth wrecchedly.

Troilus is of high degree, but though he fell into misery he did not end wretchedly; and perhaps when Chaucer called it a 'little' tragedy he did so not merely in modesty or affection, but because he felt that even in the medieval sense the story was only a minor tragedy. I have not hesitated to claim it as a comedy; in doing so I am glad to find myself in agreement with Mr Mark van Doren.

Another writer, much closer to our own time, who seems to me to have written comedies near the frontier of tragedy is Chekhov. Like Chaucer, he sympathises with his characters; but again like Chaucer he views them with the utmost detachment, as social and psychological types, and preserves the nicest balance between them, never allowing any of them to rise above or fall below the stature of common humanity. And though their environment presses heavily on them, we are mistaken if we think Chekhov meant to represent them as doomed in the way in which tragic characters are doomed; the social world in which they lived was doomed, but that is quite a different thing. So, after all, was the social world of Troilus: that of Diomede was destined to replace it. Perhaps this is the real source of the sadness of Chaucer in this great story.

The Egoist is an opposite example: Meredith called it a comedy, but surely it ought to have been a tragedy. His sympathy with both Willoughby and Clara is intense, indeed disproportionate; and Laetitia Dale's fate is even more tragic. It is hard to believe that Meredith really meant it to be anything but a tragedy, although his devotion to the idea of comedy causes him to protest, far too emphatically and far too often, that the book is comic. It has moments of high humour, as when Willoughby suddenly exclaims 'Flitch' to the astonishment of Clara. Willoughby might well have been a comic hero. Meredith rightly thought egoism the supreme subject for comedy. But there are tragic egoists: Hamlet for example.

Several of Shakespeare's plays are in the border-country between tragedy and comedy, though others conform to a strict idea of comedy. Some of these border-line plays have their own distinct classifications; for instance, *Henry IV* belongs to a regular Elizabethan class, the History Play, and should not be regarded as comedy with 'tragic' padding in between the Falstaff scenes. I cannot make up my mind about *The Merchant of Venice*, but am inclined to regard it as a tragicomedy; *Pericles* and *Cymbeline* must surely be so regarded. *Coriolanus* might be called a comitragedy. In his latest

The boundaries of comedy

plays Shakespeare was working his way back to comedy, though to a kind of play that lies, as Dr Tillyard has argued, on the other side of tragedy, but *A Winter's Tale* is in a class by itself, and Shakespeare did not get quite back to comedy until his very last complete play, *The Tempest*.

At the beginning of the eighteenth century a kind of play became popular which was called comedy, but has little right to the name; and as it still survives, both on the popular stage and more actively still in the cinema, I must give some account of the circumstances in which it came into being, and of its character. This sentimental drama was not allowed to pass unchallenged. While it was in possession of the stage, Fielding, Sterne, and Smollett kept true comedy alive in the novel; and in the 1760s Goldsmith and Sheridan recaptured the stage for comedy. Of Goldsmith's plays I have said something already. Sheridan's mixture of wit, farce, and satire and his brilliant stagecraft are surely known to all my readers; unfortunately he was himself infected with sentimentality, or made concessions to it, especially in the dénouement of *The School for Scandal*.

The sentimental drama was partly a revolt against the subject matter of Restoration Comedy, and partly a result of the rapid changes in the social structure of England at the end of the seventeenth century. Restoration Comedy was aristocratic, artificial in style, and above all intellectual. Etherege, Dryden, and Congreve were admirably rational about conduct; but fear, or at least disapproval, of emotion was a serious weakness in their standards of behaviour. The same fear is a marked characteristic of the greatest philosopher of the period, Hobbes; it has been ascribed to memories of the passion with which the political and religious conflict in the middle of the century was fought out. Whatever the cause, Restoration Comedy upon the whole views emotion with dislike and contempt. But the increasingly powerful middle class, not very strongly represented in the literature of the later seventeenth century, took the opposite view; and by the end of the century their view was beginning to predominate in England. They were rather suspicious of the intellect, after the manner of men mainly occupied in trade; and they had a low opinion of the manners and standards of Charles the Second's court. The early dissenters were not such barbarians or pedants as Butler makes out in *Hudibras*: both Milton and Marvell were of Cromwell's party, and the dissenting schools in the late seventeenth century were among the best in England. Defoe was as proud of his brains as Swift was of his; and justly so. But though the wickednesses of Restoration society have been greatly exaggerated, they had one disastrous effect: they drove puritanism and anti-intellectualism into an alliance that has proved all too durable. Pepys was far from a Puritan; he was also a man of lively intellect, and could not keep away from the theatre; but he *knew* that it was a wicked or at least a weak indulgence. Sooner or later there was bound to be an attempt to clean up the stage, the more modern and humane equivalent of suppressing it as the earlier Puritans had done. The attempt came, and in the early eighteenth century, in spite of protests, it was successful. Unfortunately it was accompanied by an upsurging of crude emotionalism which all but swept comedy away.

The first effects of this on comedy were innocent: even healthy. Congreve's plays have a greater breadth than Etherege's; and, as I have said, *The Way of the World* is the better for abandoning the Restoration pose of heartlessness. Vanbrugh, although he wrote an excellent play, *The Relapse*, to ridicule the sentimental morality that insists on converting the hero in the last act, has a strain of downright sentiment running through his plays and invigorating his style. These two writers are quite free from sentimentality. Not so Farquhar. His last play, *The Beaux' Stratagem*, is one of the most famous English comedies, and deserves its fame; but the last act is marred by a most incongruous and sinister lapse. Aimwell and Dorinda are just about to be married: they have actually got a chaplain in attendance, waiting to marry them, when Dorinda hesitates.

DORINDA Pray, my Lord, consider a little——
AIMWELL Consider! Do you doubt my Honour, or my Love?
DORINDA Neither: I do believe you equally Just as Brave—And were your whole Sex drawn out for me to choose, I should not cast a look upon the Multitude if you were absent—But, my Lord, I'm a Woman; Colours, Concealments may hide a thousand Faults in me;—Therefore, know me better first; I hardly dare affirm I know myself in anything except my Love.
AIMWELL [*aside*] Such Goodness who could injure? I find myself unequal to the Task of Villain; she has gained my Soul, and made it honest like her own—I cannot, cannot hurt her. [*aloud*] Doctor, retire. [*Exit Foigard.*] Madam, behold your Lover and your Proselyte, and judge of

my Passion by my Conversion—I'm all a Lie, nor dare I give a Fiction to your Arms; I'm all a Counterfeit, except my Passion.
DORINDA Forbid it, Heaven! A Counterfeit!
AIMWELL I am no Lord, but a poor needy Man, come with a mean, a scandalous Design to prey upon your Fortune:—But the Beauties of your Mind and Person have so won me from myself, that, like a trusty servant, I prefer the Interest of my Mistress to my own.
DORINDA Sure, I have had the Dream of some poor Mariner, a sleepy image of a welcome Port, and wake involved in Storms—Pray, Sir, who are you?
AIMWELL Brother to the Man whose Title I usurped, but Stranger to his Honour or his Fortune.
DORINDA Matchless Honesty!—Once I was proud, Sir, of your Wealth and Title, but now am prouder that you want it: Now I can show my Love was justly levelled and had no aim but Love.—Doctor, come in.

'Such goodness who could injure?' It is not merely that we can hear the gallery applaud. It is that we are in a world where generous actions and honesty are not what they seem, since we know perfectly well that the generosity will pay; its reward, indeed, follows so quickly that we suspect for a moment that Aimwell knew he was safe. But if that were so, it would not matter much; he would be all the more efficient as an adventurer. Unfortunately it is not so. He is having it both ways: the thrill of reckless virtue, and the solid reward of a pretty wife and her fortune. That is the sort of thing that must not happen in comedy; for of course it is not Aimwell but Farquhar and his audience who are having it both ways. In comedy character must be consistent. But either Aimwell was an adventurer for four acts and four scenes, and then turned into a man of feeling; or he was humbugging in the last scene; or we are to suppose that he was not really an adventurer at all, but had a heart of gold all the time, which is worst of all, for in that case Farquhar has sacrificed his play to a completely meretricious morality. The assumption is that a man who courts a woman for her money is bad (this is a sentiment foreign to the dispassionate truthfulness of Restoration Comedy); that he can make himself good by ruining in hot blood the whole plan he has made and carried through in cold blood (which merely proves him a fool or a hypocrite as well as a knave); and that Dorinda, who can hesitate to marry because 'she does not know herself', is quite right to rush into the arms of the man as soon as she knows he has no money or position, simply because he has confessed his double-dealing. And to crown everything, news arrives just after she has done so, that Aimwell's brother has died and he has succeeded to the title and fortune. Surely *she* cannot have known that she too was safe? It is too much to hope.

This would never have satisfied Congreve. His heroine would have found out the deception and punished the young man soundly; and then most likely have married him.

But it is in the plays of Steele, and particularly in *The Conscious Lovers*, that sentimental drama came to its fine flowering. It is an excellent play, given the principles on which it is written, but no more a comedy than, say, Marlowe's *Jew of Malta* is a tragedy. It is a display of naked and immoderate virtue, such as a modern English audience would not endure unless the virtue were made slightly ridiculous so as to give them the double pleasure of feeling superior to the hero and at the same time looking up to him for his 'matchless honesty'. For this modern corruption of the sentimental drama there is nothing to be said; comedy does not ridicule virtue. Steele was quite right to abandon comedy altogether; though to be sure he did not know he was doing so. He says in his preface, 'the chief Design of this [play] was to be an innocent Performance': hardly, one would think, a sufficient aim for any play. But he seems to have done himself less than justice. His chief design was probably to make his audience cry; for later in the same preface he writes 'anything that has its Foundation in Happiness and Success must be allowed to be the Object of Comedy' (this is the 'happy ending' fallacy, reduced *ad absurdum*); 'and sure it must be an Improvement of it, to introduce a Joy too exquisite for Laughter, that can have no Spring but in Delight, which is the Case of this young Lady'.

Steele was going a step further than the 'heroic' tragedies and tragicomedies of the Restoration period, which displayed the concentrated essence of virtue among princes and 'great' men, in abnormal surroundings. He brought it into ordinary society, where it looks even stranger. Almost any two or three speeches from *The Conscious Lovers* make it clear that the play is intended to be a picture of man as he should be, not man as he is; yet not man in an ideal world, but perfect man in the real world, where things can easily go wrong, and people find themselves in ridiculous or painful situations. But since all the important characters are virtuous, there is no connexion between plot and character; the two lovers are kept apart only by circumstance, which in the end has to adjust itself in

The boundaries of comedy

order to provide a happy ending. There is therefore no room for any moral except the crude and dubious one that unselfishness pays. Finally, the melodramatic ending is not simply a device for finishing the play, like the fantastic endings of most Shakespearean and Restoration Comedies: it is meant to give a thrill of elevated pleasure. The final scene of *The Conscious Lovers* may be of interest to those who have seen this sort of thing in burlesque, but never in its original seriousness.

MR SEALAND   Dear Lady! O yet one Moment's Patience: my Heart grows full with your Affliction: But yet, there's something in your story that——
INDIANA   My Portion here is Bitterness and Sorrow.
MR SEALAND   Do not think so: Pray answer me: Does Bevil know your Name and Family?
INDIANA   Alas! too well! O, could I be any other Thing than what I am—I'll tear away all Traces of my former Self, my little Ornaments, the Remains of my first State, the Hints of what I ought to have been——
   [*In her Disorder she throws away a Bracelet, which Sealand takes up and looks earnestly on it.*]
MR SEALAND   Ha! What's this? my Eyes are not deceived! It is, it is the same! the very Bracelet which I bequeathed my Wife, at our last mournful Parting.
INDIANA   What said you, Sir? Your Wife? Whither does my Fancy carry me? What means this unfelt Motion at my Heart? And yet again my Fortune but deludes me; for if I err not, Sir, your Name is Sealand: But my lost Father's Name was——
MR SEALAND   Danvers! Was it not?
INDIANA   What new Amazement! That is indeed my Family.
MR SEALAND   Know then, when my Misfortunes drove me to the Indies, for Reasons too tedious now to mention, I changed my Name of Danvers into Sealand!
   [*Enter Isabella*]
ISABELLA   If yet there wants an Explanation of your Wonder, examine well this Face (yours, Sir, I well remember) gaze on, and read in me your Sister Isabella!
MR SEALAND   My Sister!
ISABELLA   But here's a Claim more tender yet—your Indiana, Sir, your long lost Daughter.
MR SEALAND   O my Child! my Child!
INDIANA   All-gracious Heaven! is it possible? do I embrace my Father?
MR SEALAND   And I do hold thee!—These Passions are too strong for

Utterance—Rise, rise, my Child, and give my Tears their way—O my Sister! [*embracing her*].

ISABELLA   Now, dearest Niece, my groundless Fears, my painful Cares, no more shall vex thee. If I have wronged thy noble Lover with too hard Suspicions, my just Concern for thee, I hope, will plead my Pardon.

MR SEALAND   O! make him then the full Amends, and be yourself the Messenger of Joy: Fly this Instant! tell him all these wondrous Turns of Providence in his Favour! Tell him I have now a Daughter to bestow which he no longer will decline: that this Day he still shall be a Bridegroom: nor shall a Fortune, the Merit which his Father seeks, be wanting: tell him the Reward of all his Virtues waits on his Acceptance. [*Exit Isabella.*] My dearest Indiana! [*Turns and embraces her.*]

INDIANA   Have I then at last a Father's Sanction on my Love? His bounteous Hand to give, and make my Heart a Present worthy of Bevil's Generosity?

MR SEALAND   O my Child! How are our Sorrows past o'erpaid by such a Meeting! Though I have lost so many Years of soft paternal Dalliance with thee, yet, in one Day, to find thee thus, and thus bestow thee in such perfect Happiness, is ample! ample Reparation! And yet again the Merit of thy Lover!

INDIANA   O! had I Spirits left to tell you of his Actions! how strongly Filial Duty has suppressed his Love; and how Concealment still has doubled all his Obligations; the Pride, the Joy of his Alliance, Sir, would warm your Heart, as he has conquered mine.

MR SEALAND   How laudable is Love, when born of Virtue! I burn to embrace him.

INDIANA   See, Sir, my Aunt already has succeeded, and brought him to your Wishes.

[*Enter Isabella, with Sir John Bevil, Bevil junior, Mrs Sealand, Cimberton, Myrtle, and Lucinda.*]

SIR JOHN   Where! Where's this Scene of Wonder?—Mr Sealand, I congratulate, on this Occasion, our mutual Happiness—your good Sister, Sir, has with the Story of your Daughter's Fortune, filled us with Surprise and Joy! Now all Exceptions are removed: my Son has now avowed his Love, and turned all former Jealousies and Doubts to Approbation, and, I am told your Goodness has consented to reward him.

MR SEALAND   If, Sir, a Fortune equal to his Father's Hopes, can make this Object worthy his Acceptance.

BEVIL JUNIOR   I hear your Mention, Sir, of Fortune, with Pleasure, only as it may prove the Means to reconcile the best of Fathers to my Love—Let him be Provident, but let me be Happy—My ever-destined, my acknowledged Wife! [*embracing Indiana.*]

INDIANA   Wife!—O! my ever loved! my Lord! my Master!

The boundaries of comedy

SIR JOHN   I congratulate myself, as well as you, that I had a Son who could, under such Disadvantages, discover your great Merit.
MR SEALAND   O! Sir John! how vain, how weak is human Prudence! What Care, what Foresight, what Imagination could contrive such blest Events, to make our Children happy, as Providence in one short Hour has laid before us?

I have dealt at length with the sentimental drama not because of any intrinsic value it may possess, but because it throws into relief the nature of comedy, and because it has features that to this day are fathered on comedy: especially the general shape of its plot, and its irrational and irrelevant optimism about human nature and the way things turn out in the world. To sum up its ingredients, they are: the assumption that a happy ending is enough to make a play a comedy; the moral that virtue pays, and the consequent working up in the dénouement of an atmosphere of moral elation; and the attempt to depict man as he should be, but living in the world as it is, with a consequent absence of any connexion between plot and character. In this last respect particularly it is not only distinct from but directly opposite to comedy.

II

If comedy is bounded on one side by tragedy, tragicomedy, and sentimental drama, its neighbours on the other side are satire, farce, and the 'problem' play. Of these, farce is the simplest and least important; I will therefore discuss it only very briefly.

Analysing the Titania-Bottom scene in chapter 2, I found an element of farce in it; and I defined farce very roughly as physical sensationalism of a ludicrous kind, bearing the same relationship to comedy as melodrama bears to tragedy. More simply, and perhaps more accurately, it might be described as comedy with the meaning left out; which is as much as to say, with the comedy left out. Cassell's dictionary defines it as 'a short dramatic work in which the action is trivial and the sole purpose is to excite mirth'; and this indicates the main difference between it and comedy, in which the mirth is a means to an end. Thus, though farce is not comedy, comedy can contain farce, just as wine can have bubbles, though effervescence is not a generic quality of wine. Moreover farce, like soda-water, flushes and tickles without satisfying, and one does not need a discriminating palate to respond to it. Since its *sole* purpose is to excite mirth it is most likely to confine itself to merely physical situations, such as the fantasy of a man with a donkey's head on him. But clowning too is an art, and there have been clowns of genius; so there is a genius in literary clowning. Sterne possessed it, among his other qualities; the scene in *Tristram Shandy* where the hot chestnut shoots across the table and lands in the lap of Phutatorius without his noticing it is high farce. Perhaps it is also farce rather than comedy when the Shandys' baby is christened Tristram by mistake for Trismegistus, to the annoyance of his father; a *mere* pun without any meaning might be called farcical.

But it is of little use drawing out the distinction between farce and comedy into definitions and examples, because everything depends on the response of the reader or spectator. In practice one can never say with confidence 'this is comedy; that is farce'. If I think a 'comedy' lacks significance, however funny its separate episodes may be, I call it a farce; if I can see in it a significance of the kind indicated in this book I call it comedy. For me *The Importance of Being Earnest* is a farce, and *The Second Shepherd's Play* a comedy. Again, Dickens does not seem to me a writer of comedies; though it is hard to exclude Sam Weller, Betsy Trotwood, and Mr Micawber from any list of English comic characters, the ludicrous scenes in which they appear have the arbitrariness of farce, with sometimes a strong vein of sentimentality or satire. Lastly, the presence of farcical episodes or elements in real comedy complicates the distinction in practice beyond all possibility of unravelling. For example, the mistaken identities in *Twelfth Night* are a traditional device derived from late Greek comedy, through Latin comedy; yet in themselves they are farcical rather than comic. Such devices are well in keeping with a comic plot, because they contribute to a general atmosphere of fantasy in which the comic spirit can have a freer play, since it releases the characters from any pressure of relentless or inevitable circumstance.

The distinction between satire and comedy is also difficult to draw, though not for the same reason; for here there is an essential incompatibility. But as I explained in the first chapter, satire is not a clearly defined species of literature. Indeed, it originated in deliberately *formless* writing: the word means 'hotch-potch'. The Latin *satura* took at least two distinct forms; the more persistent was no more than an essay in verse. Quite early in its history it was used largely for invective, and from this historical accident the modern sense of the word is derived. What that sense is, is far from clear. It is not *mere* invective. It involves some kind of distortion: it caricatures its object, as in *MacFlecknoe*: or compares it to something ridiculous or of ill-repute, or contemptible, as usually in Pope; or stands it on its head as Samuel Butler stood Victorian England in *Erewhon*: or merely drenches it in wit as the other Samuel Butler drenched the Seventeenth-Century Puritans. One way of attacking a class of men would be to put a representative of the class into a play or novel, and give him a discreditable role in it; in Shaw's excellent comedy, *The Philanderer*, Paramore is a satire on doctors. All Peacock's novels are on the borderline between comedy and satire: perhaps in a no-man's-land. Burlesque is in a similar no-man's-land. *Joseph Andrews* begins as a burlesque of Richardson's *Pamela*: it is markedly satirical at first, but as Parson Adams becomes more prominent and Fielding's prejudice against Richardson subsides into the background, it turns into comedy. Is *The Rape of the Lock* a satirical comedy or a humorous satire? Clearly the answer depends on Pope's intention in writing the poem, which is not quite clear: unfortunately very little value can ever be placed on his own statements about his aims or motives. In this border-country it is impossible to tell simply by the effect of a book whether the author is hostile or detached: he may even not know it himself, if he is a good artist. I am disposed to give Pope the credit of having fallen in love with the scene he was depicting in this poem, and of having looked at it with the truthful vision of the comic artist, rather than with the jaundiced if penetrating eye of malice. One may draw a distinction between some of Ben Jonson's plays (for example *Cynthia's Revels* and *The Poetaster*), which are a mixture of self-advertisement and satire, and his comic masterpieces, *Volpone*, *The Alchemist*, and *Bartholomew Fair*: yet I should hardly object to the description of *Volpone* as a satire against avarice.

In spite of all this common ground, comedy and satire cannot in the last analysis be reconciled. The comic writer need not spare anything in nature, but he must not fall out with Nature herself. The satirist writes only from his own feelings; the comic writer must partly go outside his own feelings, to a conception of nature. Their techniques are in part interchangeable; but in idea they conflict. The distinction between them has something in common with the distinction between madness and sanity. Of course I do not mean to imply that all satirists are mad, or even potentially mad. Dryden and his contemporary Samuel Butler (the author of *Hudibras*) were the sanest of writers; so much so that their satire borders on comedy. But the satirist either deliberately eschews for an immediate purpose, or is helplessly cut off by his temperament from, that interplay between a man's self and the world outside him in which the life of the mind consists. The madman is, and the satirist becomes for artistic purposes, purely subjective in standpoint. The sane man is more or less capable of mental detachment; and it is by his power of detachment, or his willingness to exercise it, that the comic writer is distinguished from the satirist. Great satirists are of course more than merely angry, bitter, or disappointed men; they are usually baffled idealists. They compare life as it is with life as they would have it to be; and being unable or unwilling to reconcile the two, they attack that which is the less dear to them. But you cannot be in this position if the centre in which you take your stand is the norm; for the norm is always, by definition, reconcilable with the real. It is perhaps nowhere to be found in nature, but it is everywhere latent. Swift's Houyhnhnms are the symbols of an ideal; but they are utterly abnormal.

To return once more to Titania and Bottom. I suggested that in their love scene Shakespeare was symbolising one aspect of the curious love of eternity for the productions of time: we have fairy minds, but they are tied to the distracting, inconvenient, and sometimes grotesque behaviour of our bodies. So too the ideal and the earthy are linked together in the ludicrous and pathetic partnership of Don Quixote and Sancho Panza. Both these great comedies weigh aspiring fancy and earth-bound nature in the finest balance. Our greatest satirist, Swift, also sets them against each other in sharp relief. But his imagination cannot harmonise them; for him there is no love between time and eternity. This brings to light the fundamental difference between comedy and satire. Comedy accepts life and human nature: sometimes with a light heart, as in *A Midsummer Night's Dream*, sometimes rather sadly as in *Don Quixote*, but always with the good sense that comes from clear vision and understanding. Satire, on the other hand, does not accept; it rejects and aims at destruction; and therefore it must either direct its aim at the unnatural, or if (as in the fourth book of *Gulliver's Travels*) it is

The boundaries of comedy 141

extended to the essentials of life, it undoes its effect and becomes futile. I conclude that comedy, as well as tragedy, is not only in a different class from satire, but in a higher class; and that when a satirist develops into a comic writer his mind has become more mature and his work more truthful.

I have said that we classify a work as satirical in virtue of its immediate purpose, and that satire is distinguished from comedy by a deliberate and *ad hoc*, or an inherent and constitutional, lack of balance. The distinction between comedy and 'problem' fiction is somewhat similar. Comedy sees men as units in a society composed of similar units, and judges them accordingly. The comic dramatist does not usually give judgment himself, but he presents the evidence for a judgment by his audience; that is both better policy and better art. In order to do this he must understand human nature at least sufficiently to convince us that he knows what he is talking about, and he must be able to depict character in speech and action. But he is not only a psychologist with dramatic imagination, he is also (if only indirectly) a critic of life; and that means that if he is to do his work well he must not only know how people behave, but also have a standard of behaviour. In the best comedy these two sides, the psychological and the moral, are nicely balanced. The characters must be recognisably human, or the moral will most likely misfire. On the other hand, the dramatist must have a philosophy of life, or the play, however truthful in its detail, will lack significance and coherence, and will therefore be both dull and undramatic. This applies also to the novel, but for convenience I will discuss the question in terms of drama.

A very little philosophy will suffice to support a comedy, if it is well constructed, lively in its characterisation and incident, and well written; and for this kind of play there is a convenient name—we call it a 'light' comedy. Such are the comedies of Fletcher, which were popular throughout the seventeenth century; they have not kept the stage, but at least one of them, *Rule a Wife and have a Wife*, would be worth a revival. I suppose *She Stoops to Conquer* is a light comedy; though whether a comedy is 'light' or 'low' or 'high' must often be a matter of opinion. All these kinds of play are within the boundaries of comedy.

But a play whose human interest is merely general and not particular cannot I think properly be called a comedy. It might be (and indeed sometimes is) said that such a play, concentrating on morality or politics to the exclusion of psychology is not a drama at all, but a sermon or tract. Is not a play without interesting characters like an animal without blood or breath—a still-born infant? But there are such plays, and famous ones too. A medieval morality play is peopled by abstractions; and strange as the allegorical way of writing is to the twentieth century, *Everyman* has not lost its dramatic appeal. And another example of drama without substantial character interest is the modern Problem Play, which, in contradistinction to both comedy and tragedy, treats the situations that arise in society simply as moral or political problems, in the abstract and without reference to the indiosyncracies of human nature. There was a vogue for such plays at the end of the nineteenth and the beginning of the twentieth centuries; Galsworthy's plays belong to this class, though he called some of them comedies. But there are earlier problem plays. If we regard Shakespeare's *Measure for Measure* as a play about puritanism, and his *Troilus and Cressida* as a play about the disintegration of society in the later stages of a war, they might be classed as problem plays; characters like Isabella and Ulysses seem to owe their dramatic force to the abstractions for which they stand.

While the subject of a problem play is of intense public interest, the audience, with their minds full of their own concern in it, may be prepared to overlook its dramatic limitations; in perspective it is apt to look unreal—even more artificial and remote from life than the allegorical incidents of the *Fairy Queen*, which have at least the imagination of a poet to support them. (So, of course, by the way, have *Measure for Measure* and *Troilus and Cressida*.) But there is one condition which can give to a problem play a limited permanent interest. If the problem is complicated enough it can support a play without either psychological or emotional depth. Place a set of characters in complicated (and therefore particularised) circumstances, and they will come to life on that account alone. But no amount of ingenuity can by itself turn problem fiction into either tragedy or comedy.

Just on the other side of the boundary is the comedy of ideas. There is no reason why comedy, or for that matter tragedy, should not concern itself with social problems; but they must do so in a way compatible with their distinct natures and purposes. In theory this territory is fairly easy to map out, even if there is a difference of opinion about the side of the frontier on which any given play should be placed. Take a 'problem'—say war, or heredity. If the

The boundaries of comedy

situation is conceived as fatal—as a dilemma or disaster in which the characters are caught without hope of escape—the result is tragedy. If it is conceived as a setting for the display of character, so that the dramatist can throw a special light on a number of human types, or imaginary persons, by showing how they all react to or are influenced by a common factor in social history, the result is comedy. If on the other hand it is conceived simply as a situation, with no aim but to make the situation clear, the result is a problem play. I will give two sets of examples to illustrate these distinctions; they will, like all such examples, be hypothetical, because they depend on our interpretation of each separate work. But it does not matter; the point is as well illustrated by a hypothesis as by a known fact. In *Antony and Cleopatra* war is fatal to Antony; he knows that if he drifts or is manœuvred into war with Caesar he will surely be destroyed. And he knows also that if he stays with Cleopatra there will be war. Then 'Antony must leave her utterly'. 'Never, he will not.' This is the plot of the tragedy. In *Arms and the Man*, on the other hand, Shaw does not make his war disastrous to anybody; he merely uses it to show up the pathetic vanity and egoism of Sergius, the shrewd good-natured insignificance of Major Petkoff, the man-hunting duplicity of Raina, and the stolid and efficient romanticism of Bluntschli. It is true that he has a thesis about war—roughly, that chocolate is more useful to a soldier than bullets; but in this, as in all his best plays, he is more interested in his characters and their points of view (especially the latter), than in the thesis. He knows that human nature constantly upsets the best theories, and he is wise enough to delight in the knowledge. After all, it is Sergius who wins the battle, by disregarding all the rules of modern warfare, as Bluntschli ruefully admits. Lastly, let us suppose that *Troilus and Cressida* has no deeper purpose than I suggested in the last paragraph but one; that the central theme of the play is contained in the famous speech of Ulysses about degree, or more dramatically in the demoralisation indicated by the dry factual line, 'Hector was gone, but Helen was not up', and in the snarls of Thersites. There are ingredients of both tragedy and comedy, as surely there must be in any comprehensive picture of war; but the play as a whole will not fit into either category, and it will fit into that of the problem play. Another, and clearer, example of a problem play about war is Jean Giraudoux's *La Guerre de Troie n'aura pas lieu*.

To take the other example, heredity. This factor in human life impressed itself on the greatest European dramatist of the nineteenth century, Ibsen, so powerfully that it threw a tragic cast over the whole of his view of life. *Ghosts*, although it has much of the concern with a removable social evil proper to problem drama, is a tragedy, because its plot is founded on the notion that life is irresistibly determined, and can in spite of valiant effort be ruined, by it. This is a prominent theme of many of Ibsen's other tragedies —*The Wild Duck*, for example. Shaw, also a dramatist keenly sensitive to the current ideas of the late nineteenth century and especially to the impact of biology on ethics, a great admirer of Ibsen moreover, can never really bring himself to crush the individuality out of his characters in the ruthless manner of Ibsen. In the crisis of *Major Barbara* the fate of the heroine is in a sense determined by her heredity; she cannot resist the lure of power, and shows herself a true daughter of Undershaft, and for that matter also of Lady Britomart. But Stephen is of the same parentage and so is Sarah; and they show it in the most widely different ways, for of course heredity, though it is a problem, need not land us in fatalism. When, therefore, Barbara makes her choice, we feel it to be a real choice, taken jointly by her and Cusins of their free will and made possible by their individual temperaments. Lastly, *The Way of All Flesh*, Samuel Butler's famous *roman à thèse* (the class of novel equivalent to the problem play), is an attempt to present life in terms of biology, with no other purpose than to induce in his readers a biological approach to human character and conduct, or more specifically to education.

I am glad to end this book by these references to Bernard Shaw. He is sometimes described as a problem playwright rather than a comic dramatist. Certainly some of his plays—*Widowers' Houses*, for example, at one end, *The Apple Cart* at the other—are problem plays. But I prefer to accept his own claim, in the preface to the 1934 collection of his plays, that he is 'a classic writer of comedies' and that his purpose is 'to chasten morals with ridicule'. His characters talk a great deal about the problems of the world they and he live in, but he lets them have their separate say, and we learn more from them about the vagaries of human thought and character than about the problems they discuss. Few of our dramatists have a more impressive list of comedies to their credit than, say, *Arms and the Man, Candida, Caesar and Cleopatra, Major Barbara, Androcles and the Lion, Pygmalion,* and *St Joan*.

NOTES

Where I do not name a particular edition, the reference is to the edition named in the Bibliographical Index.

Page 6. The three quotations facing the Preface are from Johnson's *Life of Cowley* (*Lives of the Poets*, World's Classics edition, vol. i, p. 33), Coleridge's *Biographia Literaria* (ed. Shawcross, Clarendon Press, vol. ii, p. 159), and T. S. Eliot, *Notes towards the Definition of Culture* (Faber and Faber, 1948, p. 68).

Page 11, line 11. Dryden: in the *Essay of Dramatic Poesy*, 1688 (Essays, vol. i, pp. 69–70). But in *A Parallel of Poetry and Painting*, 1695, he took the opposite view (Essays, vol. ii, pp. 146–7).

Page 12, line 4. Aldous Huxley: in *Music at Night* (Chatto and Windus, 1931, p. 17).

Page 14, line 13. Aristotle: chapter 6 of the *Poetics*. The most convenient published translation of this famous work is Bywater's (ed. W. Hamilton Fyfe, Clarendon Press, 1940). I have however myself translated my quotations from Aristotle.

Page 15, line 5. '*If you believe* . . .': Meredith, *Essay*, pp. 46–7.

Page 15, line 35. Coleridge: see *Biographia Literaria*, chapter 13. 'grant me a nature having two contrary forces, the one of which tends to expand infinitely, while the other strives to apprehend or *find* itself in this infinity, and I will cause the world of intelligences with the whole system of their representations to rise up before you.' (vol. i, p. 196.) The reader must not look for an exact correspondence between Coleridge's severely metaphysical postulate and my rough generalisation.

Page 16, line 11. *Mansfield Park:* vol. iii, chapter 17, p. 461.

Page 16, line 13. Plato: in the *Republic*, Book X, 603c–607a (see the translation by Davies and Vaughan in the Golden Treasury Series, pp. 347–50).

Page 17, line 3. Blake: see his letter to Thomas Butts, 16 August 1803 (Nonesuch edition, p. 1081).

Page 18, line 4. Shylock: in *Merchant of Venice*, Act III, scene i, lines 63–4.

Page 20, line 16. Dr Johnson: see *Johnson on Shakespeare* (Oxford Miscellany, Oxford University Press, p. 17).

Page 24, line 33. '*I enter upon this speculation* . . .': Sterne, *Works*, vol. ii, pp. 174–7.

Page 37, line 7. Ben Jonson: see pages 106–7 below. The general charge that

'Shakespeare wanted art' is reported by Drummond (Jonson, *Works*, vol. i, p. 133, line 50).

Page 37, line 31. John Palmer: *The Comedy of Manners*, 1913, chapter 4, p. 139. Walpole's epigram should be read in its context (Letter to Sir Horace Mann, 31 December, 1769). It was a comment on the futility of history as a source of moral instruction. 'I have often said, and oftener think, *that this world is a comedy to those that think, a tragedy to those that feel*—a solution of why Democritus laughed and Heraclitus wept. The only gainer is History, which has constant opportunities of showing the various ways in which men can contrive to be fools and knaves. The record pretends to be written for instruction, though to this hour no mortal has been the better or wiser for it.' (Letters of Horace Walpole, ed. Mrs Paget Toynbee, Clarendon Press, 1904, vol. vii, p. 346).

Page 38, lines 28–9. Fanny Price (*Mansfield Park*); Anne Elliot (*Persuasion*); Catherine Morland (*Northanger Abbey*); Elizabeth Bennet (*Pride and Prejudice*).

Page 42, lines 11, 17. *Macbeth:* Act v, scene iii, lines 50–4; *King Lear*, Act III, scene iv, lines 28–32.

Page 44, line 10. Congreve: Dedication to *The Way of the World* (pp. 336–7).

Page 45, line 14. '*Great things are done*...': (Nonesuch edition, p. 855).

Page 46, line 36. '*Sir Edward's great object*...': chapter 8, pp. 110–12.

Page 48, line 15. '*Jones retired*...': pp. 259–61.

Page 49, line 39. The convention of courtly love: The uninformed reader may consult C. S. Lewis, *The Allegory of Love* (Oxford University Press, 1938) or (more briefly) E. M. W. Tillyard's essay on *The Testament of Cresseid* in *Five Poems* (Chatto and Windus, 1948). Both writers deal with this and many other interesting matters concerning the literature of the Middle Ages.

Page 51, line 3. Halifax: George Savile, First Marquess of Halifax, *Works*, ed. Raleigh (Oxford University Press).

Page 51, line 16. Autolycus: in *The Winter's Tale*.

Page 53, line 11. Meredith: see *Essay*, p. 11.

Page 54, line 3. '*Shakespeare always makes*...': see Johnson on *Shakespeare*, p. 15.

Page 54, last line. Shakespeare and his fellow-Elizabethans: see E. M. W. Tillyard, *The Elizabethan World Picture* (Chatto and Windus, 1943).

Page 55, line 17. The beginning of the seventeenth century: cf. page 106. For an account of this important matter, see Basil Willey, *The Seventeenth Century Background* (Chatto and Windus, 1933).

Page 55, line 27. Fletcher's realistic comedies. The best of them are *Wit Without Money*, *The Wild-goose Chase*, and *Rule a Wife and Have a Wife*.

Page 55, line 30. '*a limb of Shakespeare*': see Dryden's Preface to *Troilus and Cressida* (Essays, vol. I, p. 228).

Page 56, line 11. Etherege: for his letters, see Bibliographical Index (13).

Page 57, line 2. Jane Austen: to Anna Austen, 9 September 1814 (Letters, vol. II, p. 401).

Page 57, line 8. The death of Mrs Proudie: in *The Last Chronicle of Barset*, vol. II, chapter XXIV.

Page 59, line 7. '*Soft you*...': Act v, scene ii, lines 337–55.

Page 59, line 11. '*Henchard's lips*...': Hardy, *The Mayor of Casterbridge*, end of chapter XLIV.

Page 60, line 6. '*Sententious Mirabell!*': Congreve, *The Way of the World*, Act II, scene v, lines 43–6.

Notes

Page 60, line 10. Lady Pliant: Congreve, *The Double Dealer*, Act II, scene v, lines 78–end.

Page 60, line 25. '*Mrs Morland...*': Jane Austen, *Northanger Abbey*, chapter 1.

Page 61, line 18. The first meeting of Troilus and Criseyde: Chaucer, *Troilus and Criseyde*, Book I, lines 178–322.

Page 64, line 11. We first see her ...: in Book I, lines 106–26.

Page 64, line 27. Dryden: Preface to *Fables* (Essays, vol. II, p. 258).

Page 65, line 2. *Sentimental Journey:* in *Works*, vol. IV, pp. 68–70 ('The Translation').

Page 67, line 6. Prologue to the *Canterbury Tales:* see lines 312–13, 321–2, and 308.

Page 67, line 32. *Sanditon:* chapter 7 (p. 91).

Page 68, line 2. Darcy: in *Pride and Prejudice.*

Page 68, line 35. Chaucer's Friar ... his Monk: Prologue to the *Canterbury Tales,* lines 267, 198.

Page 68, lines 36–7. Walter Shandy—Uncle Toby—Yorick: in the passage quoted above, pp. 24–6.

Page 69, line 8. '*The Musgroves...*': chapter 5.

Page 69, last line. Criseyde's *slydynge corage:* see Book V, line 825.

Page 70, line 11. Prologue to the *Canterbury Tales,* lines 443–4; 177–83.

Page 71, line 23. '*We are told on high authority...*': p. 26.

Page 72, line 11. Byron. He is at his best in the short comic poems *Beppo* and *The Vision of Judgment,* and his long unfinished masterpiece *Don Juan.*

Pages 72–5. Quotations from *The Egoist.* "*The chief consideration...*': p. 3; '*He placed himself...*': chapter 9, p. 101; '*She walked...*': chap. 8, p. 83; '*He found himself...*': chap. 9, p. 91; '*... as he directed...*': chap. 8, p. 83; '*The presence...*': chap. 9, p. 94; '*Full surely...*': chap. 10, pp. 116–17; '*Are they not...*': chap. 11, p. 132; '*The gift...*': chap. 9, pp. 92–3; '*The tempers...*': chap. 13, p. 145; '*Marriage has...*': chap. 10, p. 102; '*Weak men...*': chap. 14, p. 157.

Page 78, line 37. *The School for Scandal:* Act II, scene i.

Page 79, line 17. Coleridge: in *Biographia Literaria,* chapter XVIII (vol. II, p. 65).

Page 80, line 10. *Much Ado:* Act V, scene iii, lines 24–7, and scene iv, lines 40–2.

Page 80, line 33. *The Tempest:* Act III, scene ii, lines 141–2.

Page 81, line 28. Benedick's soliloquy: Act II, scene iii, lines 225–46.

Page 82, line 10. John Lyly. He was also the most important English comic dramatist before Shakespeare; I think *The Woman in the Moon* is his best play.

Page 82, line 14. '*But suppose that...*': Works, vol I, pp. 206–7.

Page 83, line 18. '*The King he is...*': Act IV, scene iii, lines 1–19.

Page 84, line 10. Jaques—Portia: in *As You Like It,* Act II, scene vii, lines 139–66, and *The Merchant of Venice,* Act IV, scene i, lines 181–200.

Page 84, line 16. '*Our revels...*': Act IV, scene i, lines 148–58.

Page 85, line 24. '*Once more unto the breach*': Act III, scene i, lines 1–34.

Page 85, line 37. '*Be absolute...*': Act III, scene i, lines 5–41.

Page 87. Quotations from *As You Like It.* '*If that...*': Act I, scene iii, lines 48–51; '*Ay, now am I...*': Act II, scene iv, lines 14–16; '*I do not...*': Act II, scene v, lines 17–18; '*And your experience...*': Act IV, scene i, lines 25–7.

Page 87, line 31. '*Dost thou think...*': Act II, scene iii, lines 117–18.

Page 88, line 3. '*Courage!...*': Act I, scene ii, lines 112–14.

Page 88, line 7. '*If I had...*': Act IV, scene iii, lines 842–4.

Page 88, line 11. '*This island's mine...*': Act I, scene ii, lines 331–9.

Notes

Page 89, line 13. Meredith: see Essay, p. 17.

Page 89, line 16. *Roman de la Rose:* lines 4765–6 (see Bibliographical Index, under Chaucer).

Page 90, last line. *Love for Love:* Act II, scene iii, lines 50–95.

Page 92, line 7. Millimant. '*Mirabell, did you . . .*': from *The Way of the World*, Act II, scene iv, lines 65–112.

Page 93, line 1. '*He hits the mean . . .*': see Essay, p. 25.

Page 93, line 2. Professor Dobrée: see Bibliographical Index under Congreve; and Bonamy Dobrée, *Restoration Comedy* (Oxford University Press, 1924).

Page 93, line 24. Sir Wilful Witwoud takes off his boots: see *The Way of the World*, Act III, scene xvii.

Page 94, line 3. Sharper. '*Money is but dirt . . .*': Act II, scene i, lines 123–6.

Page 94, line 17. '*Gads-Daggers-Belts-Blades . . .*': Act II, scene i, lines 55–68.

Page 94, line 27. Sir Sampson Legend: Act II, scene vii, lines 61–71.

Page 95, line 4. '*Well, and how . . .*': from *The Way of the World*, Act IV, scene i, lines 18–37.

Page 95, line 17. Witwoud. '*Come, come . . .*': Act I, scene vi, lines 58–67.

Page 96, line 21. The *Poetics* is a treatise on tragedy. For the greater part; though there is evidence that it is incomplete in its present form. Strictly speaking, it is a treatise on fiction; for the words *poesis* and *poetike* did not mean to Aristotle exactly what the word 'poetry' means to us.

Page 99, line 1. Dr Johnson remarked . . .: see *Johnson on Shakespeare*, p. 15.

Page 99, line 6. Dryden: e.g. in the *Essay of Dramatic Poesy* (Essays, vol. I, pp. 78–80) and in the Preface to *Troilus and Cressida* (Essays, vol. I, pp. 224–8).

Page 99, line 29. Fiction is essentially philosophical: see *Poetics*, chapter 9. 'Fiction is more philosophical and of greater import than history, because fiction treats rather of universals, whereas history treats of particulars. By "universal" I mean the sort of things it is appropriate for a sort of person to say or do according to probability or necessity . . .; by "particular", what Alcibiades (for example) did or what happened to him.' See also page 118 below.

Page 100, line 23. *Aspects of the Novel:* (1927), chapter II, pp. 41–3.

Page 105, line 12. As Aristotle pointed out: in chapter 13 of the *Poetics*.

Page 108, line 13. '*language really used by men*': see Wordsworth, Preface to *Lyrical Ballads*, 1800 (*English Critical Essays, nineteenth century*, World's Classics, p. 4).

Page 108, line 30. *Everyman in his Humour:* Act III, scene iv, lines 20–2.

Page 109, line 27. *Essay on Man:* II, 133–74; elaborated in *Moral Essays*, I ('Of the Knowledge and Characters of Men').

Page 111, line 9. Singled out by Dryden: in the *Essay of Dramatic Poesy* (Essays, vol. I, pp. 79 and 83–8).

Page 112, line 24, Sir Epicure Mammon . . . His huge speech: Act II, scene ii, lines 34–94.

Page 114, line 15. preface to *The Good-Natured Man:* see *Select Works*, p. 183.

Page 116, line 1. Captain Wentworth: in *Persuasion*.

Page 119, line 29. Touchstone's famous saying: Act V, scene iv, lines 58–9.

Page 123, line 17, public opinion: see Book I, lines 84–91, and Book IV, lines 183–210.

Page 123, line 27. *Clerk's Tale:* see lines 995–1001.

Page 124, line 4. '*Pandare answerde . . .*': Book IV, lines 582–8.

Notes

Page 124, line 26. He does not want to blame her: Book V, lines 1003–9; no women ever grieved more: Book V, lines 1052–3.

Page 125, line 14. Pandarus had made a mess of his own love affairs: Book I, lines 622–3; Book II, lines 98–9 and 1105–7.

Page 125, line 26. The last talk of the two lovers: Book IV, lines 1247–1659.

Page 127, line 21. As Blake says: see *The Marriage of Heaven and Hell*, 'Proverbs of Hell', (Nonesuch edition, p. 193).

Page 129, line 26. his 'litel tragedye': see Book V, line 1768.

Page 130, line 6. Mr Mark van Doren: in *The Noble Voice* (Henry Holt & Co., U.S.A., 1946).

Page 130, line 28. Willoughby suddenly exclaims 'Flitch': chapter XI, p. 127.

Page 131, line 2. E. M. W. Tillyard, *Shakespeare's Last Plays* (Chatto and Windus, 1938), chapter II, 'The Tragic Pattern'. But I cannot agree with Dr Tillyard's contention on p. 25 that these plays are *altogether separated* from comedy in general and from Shakespeare's own earlier comedies in particular.

Page 131, line 24. Etherege, Dryden, and Congreve were admirably rational: see especially Dryden's best comedy, *Marriage à la Mode*.

Page 131, last line. The dissenting schools in the late Seventeenth Century: see James Sutherland, *Defoe* (Methuen, 1937, chapter I, pp. 17–25).

Page 132, line 6. Pepys: see his *Diary*, 31 December 1661. 'I have newly taken a solemn oath about abstaining from plays and wine . . .' But within three months he had relapsed (*Diary*, 24 March 1662).

Page 132, line 9. An attempt to clean up the stage. Its leader was not a Dissenter, but a High Church divine, Jeremy Collier (*A Short View of the Immorality and Profaneness of the English Stage*, 1698).

Page 132, line 29. Dorinda. '*Pray, my Lord . . .*': c.f. Benedick's soliloquy in *Much Ado* quoted on pp. 81–2.

Page 135, line 6. The final scene of *The Conscious Lovers:* pp. 185–7.

Page 138, line 7. *Tristram Shandy:* see vol IV, chapter 27 and chapters 14, 16 (*Works*, vol. II, pp. 86–94 and 54–9).

Page 139, line 5. *MacFlecknoe:* Dryden.

Page 143, line 12. *Antony and Cleopatra:* see Act II, scene ii, lines 238–9.

Page 143, line 29. *Troilus and Cressida:* see Act I, scene iii, lines 75–137; and Act I, scene ii, line 50.

Page 144, last line. *St Joan*. I have already indicated that I class *St Joan* as a comedy; I have not asked Mr Shaw's permission to do so, but the Epilogue seems to me to make his attitude clear.

BIBLIOGRAPHICAL INDEX

This is primarily an index of the literary and dramatic material upon which this book is based; but I have supplied dates, and arranged the authors in chronological order. For convenience of reference their names also appear in alphabetical order, in the General Index.

With regret I have come to the conclusion that it would not be helpful to my readers to specify a particular edition for each author; I have therefore only done so when I had to, for the purpose of exact page or line references in the Notes. Even the less well known works here mentioned should be available in any library that caters for students of English literature.

1 ARISTOPHANES, c. 444–380 B.C.: 12, 13, 43, 47, 109
   Birds (414), 15
   Frogs (405), 47, 109

2 PLAUTUS, T. Maccius, c. 254–184 B.C.: 13

3 TERENCE (P. Terentius Afer), ?195–?159 B.C.: 13

4 MEDIEVAL DRAMA:
   (a) *The Second Shepherd's Play* (in the Wakefield, or 'Towneley' cycle), 13, 138
   (b) *Everyman*, 142

5 CHAUCER, Geoffrey, c. 1343–1400 (Works, ed. F. N. Robinson, Houghton Mifflin Co., U.S.A., and Oxford University Press, 1933. Contains also the fourteenth-century English translation of the *Roman de la Rose*): 13, 39, 43, 45, 46, 49, 50, 55, 56, 66–7, 68, 69–70, 71, 81, 89, 93, 106, 109, 113, 114, 123, 128
   House of Fame, 43, 55
   Parliament of Fowls, 43
   Troilus and Criseyde, 45, 49–50, 55, 61–4, 66, 69, 73, 114, 123–7

Canterbury Tales, 23, 43, 50, 55, 56, 109, 114, 129; *Prologue*, 64, 67, 68, 70; *Clerk's Tale*, 123; *Nun's Priest's Tale*, 55; *Merchant's Tale*, 23, 55; *Reeve's Tale*, 49

6 CERVANTES, Miguel de, 1547–1616: 128
Don Quixote (1605), 18, 23, 38, 43, 118–19, 140

7 LYLY, John, 1554–1606 (Works, ed. R. W. Bond, Clarendon Press, 1902):
Euphues (1578), 82–3
The Woman in the Moon (c. 1591), 147

8 SHAKESPEARE, William, 1564–1616 (Complete Works, ed. Craik, Oxford University Press, 3 vols.: Comedies, 1911; Histories and Poems, 1911; Tragedies, 1912): 12, 18–19, 20–1, 36–7, 38, 41–2, 43, 44, 46, 53–5, 56, 59, 76, 78, 79–88, 93, 94, 96, 99, 105–6, 107, 108, 109, 111–12, 117, 118, 119, 128, 130–1, 135, 142, 143
The Comedy of Errors (?1593), 83
Love's Labour's Lost (?1593), 83–5
A Midsummer Night's Dream (?1595), 14, 20–4, 38–9, 43, 53, 79, 87, 99, 108, 109, 111, 119, 137, 140
The Merchant of Venice (?1596), 84, 85, 105, 130
Much Ado About Nothing (c. 1598), 20, 23, 32, 80, 81–2, 83, 84, 111
As You Like It (c. 1599), 23, 80, 83, 84, 87, 96, 98, 99, 111, 119
Twelfth Night (c. 1602), 18, 23, 80, 87, 138
All's Well that Ends Well (c. 1603), 96
Measure for Measure (?1604), 43, 83, 85–6, 88, 142
The Winter's Tale (?1611), 51, 88, 107, 131
The Tempest (?1611), 18, 55, 80, 84, 85, 88, 96, 99, 107, 108, 119, 131

9 JONSON, Ben, 1573–1637 (Works, ed. Herford and Simpson, Clarendon Press, 1925 and onwards): 37, 43, 44, 55, 80, 89, 99, 106–14, 119, 128, 129, 139
Everyman in his Humour (1598), 44, 80, 107, 108, 112
Everyman out of his Humour (1599–1600), 108–9
Volpone (1606), 19, 51, 105, 111–12, 115, 139
Epicoene, or The Silent Woman (1609), 111, 112
The Alchemist (1610), 105, 112–14, 139
Bartholomew Fair (1614), 55, 106, 112, 139

10 FLETCHER, John, 1579–1625 (Published under the title 'Beaumont and Fletcher'): 55, 110, 141
Wit without Money (?1614), 146
The Wild-goose Chase (?1621), 146
Rule a Wife and Have a Wife (1624), 141, 146

11 MOLIERE, Jean-Baptiste POQUELIN, 1622–1673: 13, 115, 128
Le Misantrope (1666), 18–19, 38, 45

12 DRYDEN, John, 1631–1700: 89, 131, 140
Marriage à la Mode (1672), 148
Essays (ed. W. P. Ker, Clarendon Press, 2 vols., 1900) 11, 55, 64, 99, 111

Bibliographical Index

13 ETHEREGE, Sir George, ?1634–1690: 50, 51, 56, 89, 131, 132
    The Letter-book of Sir George Etherege (ed. Sybil Rosenfeld, Oxford University Press, 1928), 56

14 WYCHERLEY, William, 1640–1715 (Works, ed. Montague Summers, Nonesuch Press, 1924): 50, 51, 89, 93, 110
    The Plain Dealer (?1672–3), 50
    The Country Wife (1673), 50, 51, 52–3

15 VANBRUGH, Sir John, 1664–1726: 51, 132
    The Relapse (1696), 132

16 CONGREVE, William, 1670–1729 (Comedies, ed. Bonamy Dobrée, World's Classics): 44, 51, 58–9, 72, 76, 78, 81, 83, 89–95, 110, 117, 128, 131, 132, 134.
    The Old Bachelor (1693), 93–4
    The Double-dealer (1694), 60, 94, 120
    Love for Love (1695), 90–1, 93, 94–5
    The Way of the World (1700), 20, 44, 58, 60, 89–90, 91–2, 93, 94, 95, 117, 119–20, 132

17 ADDISON, Joseph, 1672–1719: 71, 89
    The Spectator (1711–12), 56

18 STEELE, Sir Richard, 1672–1729:
    The Conscious Lovers (1722; in Eighteenth Century Comedy, ed. W. D. Taylor, World's Classics), 134–7

19 FARQUHAR, George, 1678–1707: 50
    The Beaux' Stratagem (1707; in Eighteenth Century Comedy, World's Classics), 132–4

20 POPE, Alexander, 1688–1744: 72, 89, 109, 139
    The Rape of the Lock (1712), 139

21 FIELDING, Henry, 1707–1754 (Novels, Basil Blackwell, 1926): 43, 45, 62, 70–1, 110, 114, 128, 131
    Joseph Andrews (1742), 139
    Jonathan Wild (1743), 71
    Tom Jones (1749), 23, 45, 48–9, 70, 98, 111, 115, 121–2, 125

22 STERNE, Laurence, 1713–1768 (Works, Shakespeare Head Edition, Blackwell, 1926): 46, 61, 62, 64–6, 78, 110, 117, 128, 131
    Tristram Shandy (1759–67), 14, 24–6, 38, 39, 56–7, 68, 115, 119, 138
    A Sentimental Journey through France and Italy (1768), 65–6, 70

23 SMOLLETT, Tobias, 1721–1771: 131

24 GOLDSMITH, Oliver, 1728-1774 (Select Works, ed. A. W. Pollard, Macmillan, 1901): 46, 78, 110, 114-15, 128, 131
The Vicar of Wakefield (1766), 56
The Good-natured Man (1769), 114-15
She Stoops to Conquer (1773), 56, 98, 114, 115, 141

25 SHERIDAN, Richard Brinsley, 1751-1816: 46, 78, 131
The School for Scandal (1777), 78-9, 131

26 AUSTEN, Jane, 1775-1817 (The Novels, ed. R. W. Chapman, Oxford University Press, 3rd edition, 1933): 37, 39, 43, 46-7, 61, 67-9, 71, 76-8, 81, 89, 110, 115-16, 128
Northanger Abbey (1803-18), 38, 61, 69, 115-16
Pride and Prejudice (1813), 14, 20, 38, 46, 68, 69, 78, 98, 115-16
Mansfield Park (1814), 16, 38, 46
Emma (1816), 22, 26-31, 38, 39, 68, 76-8, 115-16, 122-3, 125, 127
Persuasion (1816-18), 38, 46, 69, 115-16
Sanditon: fragment of a novel written January to March 1817 (Clarendon, Press, 1925), 46-7, 67
Letters, collected and ed. R. W. Chapman (Clarendon Press, 1932), 57

27 LAMB, Charles, 1775-1834: 71

28 PEACOCK, Thomas Love, 1785-1886: 139
The Four Ages of Poetry (1823), 11

29 Lord BYRON, George Gordon, 1788-1824: 72
Beppo (1818), 147
Don Juan (1819-24), 147
The Vision of Judgment (1822), 147

30 DICKENS, Charles, 1812-1870: 138
Pickwick Papers (1836-7), 138
David Copperfield (1849-50), 138

31 TROLLOPE, Anthony, 1815-1882: 57
The Last Chronicles of Barset (1866): 57

32 MEREDITH, George, 1827-1909 (The Surrey Edition, Times Book Club, 1912): 57, 72-6, 110
Essays on the idea of Comedy and of the uses of the Comic Spirit (1877), 14-15, 43, 53, 89, 93
The Egoist (1879), 72-5, 118, 130

33 WILDE, Oscar, 1856-1900:
The Importance of Being Earnest (1895), 138

Bibliographical Index

34 SHAW, George Bernard, 1856–1950: 13, 24, 36–7, 39–40, 46, 57, 86, 110, 128
143–4
Widowers' Houses (1892), 36, 144
The Philanderer (1893), 139
Arms and the Man (1894), 143, 144
Candida (1895), 45, 144
Caesar and Cleopatra (1898), 144
Major Barbara (1905), 20, 32–7, 38, 39–40, 144
Androcles and the Lion (1912), 144
Pygmalion (1912), 44, 144
St Joan (1923), 39, 127, 144, 149

35 CHEKHOV, Anton Pavlovich, 1860–1904: 130

36 BEERBOHM, Sir Max, 1872–1956 (Uniform Edition, Heinemann, 1922): 71
Yet Again (1909), 9, 18
Seven Men (1919), 19
Lytton Strachey: the Rede Lecture, 1943 (Cambridge University Press), 71

GENERAL INDEX

Names and titles are in italics, subjects in Roman type. Authors and works preceded by a numeral in brackets are indexed under that number in the Bibliographical Index.

(17) *ADDISON*
Aeschylus, 13
Aesop, 43
Affectation, 15, 44, 110, 120
Allegory, 12, 38, 43, 99, 142
Architecture, 10
(1) *ARISTOPHANES*
Aristotle, 12, 15, 96–9, 117–18, 127, 129
Art, 9, 15, 19, 30, 36–7, 41, 58, 99, 103–4, 105, 111, 141
Artificiality, 111, 131, 142
Athens, 12–13
(26) *AUSTEN, Jane*

Bacon, Francis, 106
(36) *BEERBOHM, Sir Max*
Belloc, Hilaire, 19
Blake, William, 17, 45, 129
Bracegirdle, Mrs, 58
Brontë, Emily, 72
Bunyan, John, 44
Burlesque, 80, 134, 139
Butler, Samuel (1612–80), 131, 139
Butler, Samuel (1835–1902), 139, 140, 144
(29) *BYRON*

Caricature, 43, 140
(6) *CERVANTES*
Character, 43, 44–5, 61, 93, 96–8, 105–17, 129, 133, 134, 137, 139, 141, 142, 143, 144
Charles II, 19, 50, 131
(5) *CHAUCER*
(35) *CHEKHOV*
Christianity, 17, 98
Civilisation, 15, 45, 104
Clair, René, 129
Coleridge, 6, 15, 72, 79
Collier, Jeremy, 149
Comedy of Humours, 37, 108–17
Comedy of Manners, 37, 110
Comic Microcosm, 56–7
Comic Relief, 36
Common sense, 15, 29, 79, 87–9
(16) *CONGREVE*
Convention, 49, 104, 110, 116–17, 129
Crime, 44
Cynicism, 51, 62, 125

Death, 17, 19
Definitions, 14, 100
Defoe, 132

Description, 62–7, 68–9, 71, 81
Destiny, 16, 17, 98
Detachment, 40, 42, 61, 130, 140
Dialogue, 61, 76–9, 81, 93
(30) DICKENS
Dissenters, 131
Dobrée, Bonamy, 93, 148
Domestic Comedy, 56
Donne, 74
Drama, 10, 58, 77, 78, 86, 87, 93, 97, 119, 141–2
(12) DRYDEN

Eccentricity, 17, 18, 43, 45, 105, 109
Egoism, 74, 114, 130
Eighteenth century, 56, 109, 110, 112, 131, 132
Eliot, T. S., 6
Elizabethan Age, 13, 55, 81, 83, 106, 112
Epic, 10–11, 12, 57
Essay, 10, 71
(13) ETHEREGE
Ethics, 37, 103–4, 110, 123
Euripides, 47
Evans, Dame Edith, 59
(4b) 'Everyman'
Experience, 116, 117

Fable, 43, 97–8, 99–100
Farce, 22, 36, 44, 60, 131, 137–8
(19) FARQUHAR
Feeling, 30, 38, 100, 131, 142
Fiction, 96–105, 148
(21) FIELDING
(10) FLETCHER
Folly, 44, 94, 113, 120, 127
Fops, 117, 120
Forster, E. M., 100

Galsworthy, John, 142
Generalisation, 103, 128
Gibbon, 71
Giraudoux, Jean, 143
(24) GOLDSMITH
Good nature, 89–90, 115, 117, 120, 125
Greek drama, 12, 13, 97–8, 138

Halifax, Lord, 51
Happy ending, 11, 18–20, 134–5, 137
Hardy, Thomas, 59, 72, 73, 121
Hero, 102, 113–14, 115–17
Heroic drama, 134
History plays, 85, 87, 130
Hobbes, 131
Humour, 9, 36, 40, 130. See also Comedy of Humours
Huxley, Aldous, 12

Ibsen, 13, 144
Ideal and real, 24, 45, 134, 140
Ideas, 37, 42, 55, 57, 102–5, 128, 142–3
Imagery, 60, 81, 88
Imagination, 16, 53, 54, 66–7, 68, 70, 71–2, 79, 85, 100, 102, 105, 111, 123, 125, 140, 141, 142
Inductive method, 128, 129
Innuendo, 52–3, 70
Internal comedy, 32, 82–4, 116, 126
Irony, 22, 23, 24, 30–1, 36, 69–71, 72, 74, 75–6, 77, 100, 123
Italy, 83

Johnson, Samuel, 6, 20, 53, 99
(9) JONSON, Ben
Joyce, James, 57
Judgment, 51, 91, 105, 106, 116, 124–5, 141

(27) LAMB
Language, 11, 76
Latin comedy, 13, 83, 138
Laughter, 6, 10, 15, 17–18, 22, 40, 127, 134
Lewis, C. S., 146
Life, 99, 101–5, 121, 141
(7) LYLY
Lyric, 10, 96

Manners, 62, 78, 105. See also Comedy of Manners
Marlowe, Christopher, 105, 134
Marriage, 19–20, 96
Marvell, Andrew, 131
Melodrama, 22, 105, 135, 137
(32) MEREDITH

General Index

Metaphor, 73, 93, 100
Middle Ages, 13, 62, 108, 127, 129
Milton, 19, 51, 131
Misunderstanding, 44
Modes of thought, 10, 110
Modesty, 16
(11) *MOLIERE*
Moralising, 62
Morality, 26, 47, 51-2, 56, 105, 113-14, 132, 133, 134-5, 137, 141, 144
Morality plays, 43, 142

Nashe, Thomas, 83
Nature, 9, 15, 18, 24, 30, 41, 44, 46, 85, 99, 104, 106, 114, 119, 120, 121, 137, 139-41, 142
Norm, 17, 19, 29, 41-3, 46, 50, 105, 116, 140
Novel, 10, 12, 31, 61, 67, 71, 72, 77, 100, 102, 103, 115

Palmer, John, 37
Parable, 99
(28) *PEACOCK*
Pepys, 132
Philosophy, 14, 17, 42, 89, 99, 103, 106, 141
Plato, 16
(2) *PLAUTUS*
Playfair, Sir Nigel, 59, 93
Plot, 18-19, 96-9, 114, 117-27, 129, 134, 137
Poetry, 6, 9, 24, 53, 59, 68, 72, 78, 79-84, 85, 93, 108, 148
(20) *POPE*
Pride, 16
Probability, 117-19, 121, 148
Problem plays, 36, 37, 137, 141
Proportion, 15, 39, 41, 121, 127, 130
Psychology, 14, 16, 17, 37, 93, 99, 105, 108-10, 141, 142

Racine, Jean, 13
Realism, 43, 53, 55, 57, 100, 105, 106-8, 119
Restoration Drama, 46, 50-3, 56, 89, 110, 116, 120, 131-2, 133, 135

Rhetoric, 79, 84-6
Rhythm, 60, 88, 93
Richardson, Samuel, 139
Rochester, Lord, 51
Roman de la Rose, 43, 89
Romance, 45

Satire, 10, 36, 60, 72, 78, 90, 106, 113, 131, 137, 138, 139-41
Science, 103, 110, 128
Scott, Sir Walter, 67
Seneca, 13
(4a) *Second Shepherd's Play*
Sentiment, 45
Sentimentality, 50, 57, 106, 114, 131-7, 138
Seventeenth century, 50-1, 55, 93, 106, 110, 111, 131-2
Sex, 45-53
(8) *SHAKESPEARE*
(34) *SHAW, G. B.*
Shelley, 16, 51
(25) *SHERIDAN*
Simile, 64, 94
(23) *SMOLLETT*
Social feeling, 17, 41
Society, 6, 40, 51, 53-7, 88, 104, 105, 130, 141
Soliloquy, 32, 82-4, 93, 119
Sophocles, 12
Spenser, Edmund, 142
(18) *STEELE*
(22) *STERNE*
Stories, 58, 60, 99-102, 117, 119-20, 121
Strindberg, August, 13
Style, 22, 29, chapter 4, 129
Subject matter, 18, chapter 3, 129
Surprise, 110, 111
Sutherland, James, 149
Swift, Jonathan, 71, 89, 132, 140
Symbolism, 22, 24, 38, 54, 99
Sympathy, 18, 36, 38-9, 100, 105, 106, 112, 130

Taste, 88
(3) *TERENCE*
Thought, 38

Tillyard, E. M. W., 131, 146
Tradition, 41
Tragedy, 9, 10–11, 12–13, 14, 15–16, 18, 19, 22, 29, 36, 37, 38, 40, 41–2, 45, 58–9, 73–5, 79, 88, 96–9, 104, 105, 106, 110, 111, 117–18, 122, 124, 127, 129–30, 141, 143–4
Tragicomedy, 11, 130
(31) *TROLLOPE*
Twentieth century, 12, 108, 127, 142

(15) *VANBRUGH*
van Doren, Mark, 130
Victorian Age, 50, 57, 72

Walpole, Horace, 37–8
(33) *WILDE*
Willey, Basil, 146
Wit, 9, 79, 81–3, 87, 88–9, 93–4, 117, 131
Wordsworth, William, 108
(14) *WYCHERLEY*